MY MISERABLE SEARCH FOR ENLIGHTENMENT

MY MISERABLE SEARCH FOR ENLIGHTENMENT

A QUEST FOR GOD AND THE ETERNAL SELF

MARK SHELLEY KENZER

LIONCREST
PUBLISHING

MY MISERABLE SEARCH FOR ENLIGHTENMENT
A Quest for God and the Eternal Self

FIRST EDITION

ISBN   978-1-5445-3615-6 *Hardcover*
       978-1-5445-3613-2 *Paperback*
       978-1-5445-3614-9 *Ebook*

Some names in this book have been changed to protect individuals' privacy.

CONTENTS

INTRODUCTION

I WAS NINE WHEN MY LITTLE BROTHER ROSS—THE MOST sensitive and imaginative of my brothers—mentioned at the dinner table that he couldn't fall asleep at night. There was a moon, he insisted, that was lighting up the bedroom we shared every night when he went to bed. This moon had no source of light. It simply glowed, and it disappeared by the time my older brother, Paul, and I went to bed.

"Tell them what you told me," my mother urged him. And Ross, obliging, admitted that this mysterious light scared him.

Paul and I agreed to go to bed with him that night and straighten everything out.

At the dinner table, it seemed a simple thing to ease his mind, although I should have known better. Even at my young age, I'd come to recognize that my family was different from others. Some of us had a connection to a deeper reality. And while I was by far the most affected by this connection, Ross also had a sense of truth beyond everyday material life.

But I was nine, and I wasn't yet completely aware of my own experiences or what they meant. So as we sat down on Ross's bed and faced the dresser across the room, I still assumed it must all be some kind of practical joke.

I was quickly proven wrong.

Before our eyes, a golden-orange harvest moon with big craters rose from behind the dresser. It was three feet across. Though none of us had ever seen the moon up close at that point, we knew this was an actual moon in our bedroom. There appeared to be no source for the light. There was no lamp on the dresser. The shades were pulled, and the curtains were closed on the windows. And anyway, our house was on a dead-end street with no streetlights, and no cars were passing outside. There were no tools or toys that could create that moon back then. The light was self-generating.

This shimmering warm light did not remain stationary. Instead, true to Ross's description, it rose like a moon, crossed the ceiling, and began to set behind our heads, making its way on the floor directly in front of us. My brothers and I got down from the bed and tried to make shadows in its radiance. We put hands and feet over the light—we stood in the craters—but we had no effect upon it. The light shined undiminished.

Eventually, this moon went back under the dresser and disappeared.

A PEEK AT A DEEPER TRUTH

You might assume that such a story is the product of imaginative, innocent children. After all, a shimmering harvest moon crossing a child's room isn't supposed to be physically possible. It seems to belong more in a book of fairy tales than a memoir. But this is only one of the many miraculous experiences that have filled my life and will fill these pages.

Over the sixty-plus years I have lived my present life, I have battled the Devil and encountered Jesus; spoken with the dead and seen the future; built a million-dollar company and faced decades in jail; and felt spiritual forces so intensely, they took a toll on my heart.

Over that time, I have lived the sort of life that some assume only occurs in fiction and others believe only happened in the distant past. Having actually experienced it, I can tell you, it is all very real and very present. Some of it sucked. But some of it was transcendent.

This is the story of all of it: a story of tragedy, pain, and betrayal, as well as a glance at the real truth of existence, one that goes beyond our everyday encounters.

THE FACE IN THE BATHROOM MIRROR

These transcendent experiences can be a burden, but they have also provided me with a clarity about our place in the cosmic order that others are missing. Surviving abuse, betrayal, and severe loss, I had to work hard not to be an angry, violent, or depressed person. It wouldn't have been surprising if I had been suicidal—as, indeed, I was at one point.

What made the difference was that connection with what for others is unseen.

As a kid, I would go to the bathroom, lock the door, and place my feet in the sink while I ran the water over them. I would play in the water and dwell on how sad I was. Because I'd been sickly as an infant, I never received the tactile love from my mother that newborns need. My parents hit me regularly and never said they loved me.

They were hard years, and I was a lonely child haunted by chronic nightmares.

In the bathroom, I would finally allow myself to cry. On one particular occasion, though, I looked in the mirror and I saw not the red, wet face of a miserable young boy, but a stranger's face with a kindly set of eyes staring right into mine. I had no idea who this was—I had certainly never seen him before. It wouldn't be until adulthood that I fully understood this was what the *Bhagavad-gita* called the "Super-Soul," or what a Christian might call the Holy Spirit.

All I understood then was that the face looking back at me made me feel better. I knew that everything would be okay. There was no promise that this presence would make the pain go away or my struggles end, but it filled me with comfort all the same to know that someone was there with me, like a witness.

None of this insight kept me from a life full of mistakes. Like most people, I went searching for simple answers, easy solutions, and quick access to the Divine. I wanted God to do all the work for me. What my journey suggests, though, is that truth is far more complex, and if you want to experience it, you have to do the work yourself. You have to undo your own illusions and pull away the pieces of the projected reality you have created. Saints like Moses, Jesus, Buddha, Muhammad, or Sri Krishna can point a way, but each of us must find the path and choose to walk it ourselves.

This is the story of my efforts to walk that path. And in it, I hope I can help point the way for all who are interested.

WHAT IS WAKING UP?

In that moment in the mirror, I knew I was not who I thought I was. For an instant, I saw the eternal.

Everyone goes through these crises, but most people push them away. They go out to make more money, find a new spouse, or buy a fancy car. They fear the truth. They prefer the stories they tell themselves.

Enlightenment is when the story stops, and the truth frees us from cycles of rebirth and pain. Waking up is seeing things as they really are and accepting what they are and what they are not. The material world is entirely temporary. Birth means death. All connections break; all objects are impermanent. We do not want to face this. So we constantly project a false reality—a sense of self that only exists in our stories and in the stories of others. Our greatest fear is to accept "what is," and our worst addiction is to these stories.

When I asked my mother if I would die, she told me the standard answer: "Yes, but not for a long time, so don't worry." But we should worry.

Material life is an inherently meaningless and temporary story. My life proves that over and over again—as may yours. Rebirth means another meaningless and temporary bodily story. Only through enlightenment can we free ourselves from the body, the temporary, and our isolation from the Divine.

One day, if it hasn't happened already, the realization will drop upon you that you haven't been living an authentic life. Rather, "life" has been living you.

Realizations like this are the start of connecting to something big, eternal, and real. This is Self-Realization. It is the journey I have taken all my life.

Your body is temporary, but your soul is not. When your current body wears itself out, your soul finds a new body. This is called rebirth or reincarnation. The soul is simply changing bodies. We are all aware that we are the same person who occupied our body in elementary school, the person who occupied it in high school, and the person who is still occupying it now. Though events are taking place, the soul remains the same. In this continuous cycle, you die, and then you take birth again and again and again. But you can transcend this and connect back to the Divine. Everything continues on, and you can wake up and see beyond your material nature and into the eternal.

You can, as the Psalmist says, "Be still and know that I am God."

THE DOOR IS OPEN

In my childhood, my mother had a dream. She dreamed that the whole world was watching me. Many years later, a friend introduced me to Fathai, the abbot at a Buddhist temple in Portland. After meditating together, he pulled me aside. "Mark," he said, "I know that life has been very hard for you, and I want to tell you that you have to keep up your practice, it is going to get easier. I meditated on your life and I can see that you are going to help a lot of people. Not just thousands, but hundreds of thousands—I have seen it. You are going to help them with your writings, so don't give up."

That is my aim in this book. To help as many as possible through the story of my hardships and the transcendence I have found through my spiritual practices and gifts.

In the *Bhagavad-gita*, Krishna says, "I am seated in everyone's heart, and from Me come remembrance, knowledge, and forgetfulness."

It is up to each of us to choose whether we wish for God to help us remember and gain knowledge or else forget. According to the original founder of the Hare Krishna movement, Sri Chaitanya Mahaprabhu, we are all "inconceivably simultaneously in oneness and difference" with the Absolute, or God. We are on a spectrum in which we swing from being one with the Absolute and individual. Due to our minute independence, we have the freedom to choose how we swing. And we are tasked to cultivate both understandings of ourselves.

These truths are recognized by all the great spiritual leaders from across the world. They underpin Buddhism, Hinduism, Christianity, Islam, and Judaism. As Jesus said, "Behold, I stand at the door, and knock: if any man hear my voice, and open the door, I will come in to him, and will sup with him, and he with me."

Through this book, I am showing the direction to that door. The story ahead is complex, disruptive, upsetting, and triumphant. It's messy, as all life is, but also emphatic in its lessons. It is my story, but one that points in the direction we must all travel. It is for you to choose to walk it or not.

CHAPTER 1

THE MONSTERS COMING WITH ME

I SUFFERED FROM HORRIFIC NIGHTMARES THROUGHOUT my childhood. They were there from my earliest days. Sometimes, I dreamt of being tortured.

It was rare as a child to open my eyes from a night's sleep and not have a family member at my bedside, trying to wake me up. If they succeeded, it signaled it had been a good night, and I felt excited and relieved. Usually, though, I remained asleep despite their attempts.

My parents would walk in and out of my room for hours while I violently thrashed around my bed or sleepwalked. Sometimes, my brothers would pull up chairs and sit and watch as I jumped out of bed and ran around the room yelling.

A number of times, in my sleep, I tried to climb up into my brother Paul's bed, who slept on the top of our set of bunk beds.

"Get back into your own bed, Mark!" he would say, trying to wake me while simultaneously shoving me to the floor. I would simply bounce up from the floor into my bed, unphased from the fall and still asleep.

Whenever I finally did wake, I'd be coated in sweat, my

pajamas soaked. I'd find my sheets on the ground, having been tossed from the bed during my rage and restlessness.

These dreams haunted me.

One time, I was curled up under my bed, hiding, amidst a dream that I was in a dungeon. A huge man was trying to get me and drag me out of my cell. I cowered in the corner, the man's fingertips within an inch of grasping my foot. The dream went in and out as my mind toggled between awake and asleep, awake and asleep.

"Mark, it's me!"

I could hear my mother's voice in the distance. Still, I continued to drift in and out of my nightmare for several minutes. As her voice became louder, I began to make out her face. She was under the bed, trying her best to pull me out.

"Mark, it's me!"

Slowly, she came into my reality. Once I realized it was her, I let her pull me out.

There was no relief from these dreams.

They happened even when I dozed off while watching TV. I'd shoot up from the couch yelling, "It's all your fault!" pointing to an invisible figure in front of me. The dream would wake me enough that I ran up to bed to sleep for the rest of the night, but I never fully escaped it.

You might think you're simply reading about a troubled child, that I needed to see a psychologist or therapist. However, there was more to the story than a little boy with chronic nightmares. My early life was full of signs of the battles and experiences that were ahead. These dreams were just one manifestation.

When I experienced these dreams, I was in what Tibetan Buddhists call the bardo state, in the space between death and rebirth. My nightmares revealed to me how I had come out of death and into new life over many lifetimes. It was like I had residue left over from my previous lives.

I dreamt once that I was in a war and I was shot. I left my body and all of these little winged, naked creatures started tearing all the flesh and sinews off my body and eating them. It was only later that I realized for all their hideousness, they were actually helpful. They were removing my old attachments.

We all, to some degree, go through these states, either within our dreams or during other periods of unconsciousness. Some are just more sensitive to them than others.

I have always been extremely sensitive to the spiritual realities around me. Where most people lose their memories of previous lives in the dying process, mine clung to me through dreams. My awareness of various spiritual states from a young age and throughout my life allowed me to have a direct connection with the spiritual world most don't have. They told me things about my life that would otherwise have remained a mystery—and they have always brought me closer to spiritual realities that remain invisible to most. They also, however, made it painful for me to fully enter this life—and it was a life already filled with plenty of pain.

BORN SICK

When my mother was eight months pregnant with me, she fell down a flight of stairs. I later found out she was convinced she damaged me. I unknowingly carried that worry into my life.

I was born on March 11, 1957, with my body covered with boils. Boils use your blood, and so I would need five pints of blood to stay alive. Doctors didn't believe I would make it. In memories I recovered years later through meditation (and which my mother confirmed), I could hear the words, *you are going to die.*

Because of these boils, my mother couldn't hold me or nurse me. For the first month, I did nothing but scream. I wouldn't even drink formula—all I could take in was warm water with a little honey.

This start in life meant that I never truly learned intimacy. Because I was so ill, I didn't experience the sense of safety and deep connection that comes from a newborn's contact with its mother. This created a disconnect that has lasted my whole life.

Being born sick caused a unique beginning in my life spiritually, as well. As my friend, the therapist Bill Welch, would point out to me as an adult, the trauma I went through in infancy likely caused me to jump out of my consciousness into another realm. I would spend years reintegrating into this reality, filling in the pieces of this life that were missing because I spent time in other realms as an infant and child.

Slowly, the boils went away, although I still had scars long into childhood, but that was not the end of my health issues.

At around four years old, I developed severe sinus problems. I'm not exaggerating when I say I truly put new meaning into the term "snot-nosed kid." Green snot was everywhere—on my clothes, on the bedposts, and on the wall behind my bed. I didn't even realize I was doing it, but I would just wipe it everywhere as I slept because I couldn't breathe.

When I'd wake up in the morning, my eyes would be sealed shut with mucus. I'd have to walk blindly to the bathroom and splash hot water over my face until I could see.

These sinus problems gave me severe daily headaches and migraines that occurred about once a month. During these migraines, which may have actually been ministrokes, half of my body would go numb, including half of my tongue. Half of my brain would shut down, too. I could recognize people but couldn't say their name. Whenever I had a migraine, I had extreme sensitivity to light and sound, as well. A car passing by sounded like it was right next to me.

To add to my sinus issues, my first teeth were green because my mother took Tetracycline while pregnant. My eyes had black circles around them from not sleeping—both because I couldn't breathe and because of my nightmares. These ailments wouldn't be the only obstacles comprising my childhood. I endured additional traumas from my family that would make a lasting impact on the rest of my life.

A TROUBLED FAMILY

I inherited a strong Jewish genetic karma of suffering and struggle. In response to this karma, my family has always been split between scientific thinkers and spiritual journeyers.

On one side, there was my father, Jerry, a technical mastermind who basically invented the conference phone. When he worked for MARS signal company as a young man, he developed the rotating siren, which would be sold all around the world for emergency vehicles.

A man of average height whose curly hair had turned gray and begun to thin by the time I came along, Dad had created all sorts of inventions—although, unfortunately, he didn't own any of the patents. During my childhood, I watched him tooling away on inventions with a glint in his robin-egg blue eyes. That conference telephone he created for the family was more advanced than what you could get on the market for business in those days. He also invented a gun that fired a beam of light that we used to knock over toy soldiers. He was full of million-dollar inventions, but we couldn't afford to bring any of them to the market. It wasn't until the early '70s that he started to make his fortune. This was the time that laundromats in strip malls became popular. Dad worked as an electrical contractor, mostly for PWS, and did all the wiring for those shopping centers in California.

Norma and Jerry married on March 13, 1949

Others noticed Dad's brilliance, too. My brother, Paul, tells a story about when he worked as a server at a high-end restaurant and waited on the three men Dad worked for at PWS. Paul overheard their conversation about a man they deemed a "super genius."

Paul couldn't help but ask who they were talking about. "Jerry Kenzer," they replied.

As humble and hardworking as Dad was, though, he had a dark side.

First, money was everything to my father, and he had a very strained relationship with it. For all of Dad's money, he never wanted to spend any of it—not on us, not even on himself. He only had two pairs of work clothes—one clean and one in the wash. He wouldn't buy himself a new car unless it made him money, such as a utility truck for work.

I realized later that my dad's tightfistedness was because of his own father, who had immigrated to America from Poland under fire, in a small rowboat, with nothing except his small savings sewn into the leg of his pants pocket so it wouldn't be lost or stolen. My grandfather came over on a ship, earning a small amount for watching over the horses on board. When he arrived in America in 1913, he was just seventeen years old. Disembarking, he only received half his payment, and sensing he'd get no more, left to make it in this new country.

Grandpa told me incredible, terrifying stories of his struggle to survive. He'd sleep in cold, damp basements. One time, he woke up and a big sewer rat was gnawing on a sore on his arm. For years, my dad watched his father struggle to make ends meet.

My dad also learned to be violent and abusive from my grandfather. Grandpa was a huge, powerful, brute of man who used his force to discipline my father and his brothers harshly during their childhood. To visualize just how large my grandfather was, he claimed to be able to carry two 300-pound blocks of ice at once. I myself witnessed him move a baby grand piano out of our house—by himself.

My father, in turn, practiced these same methods for discipline, albeit with a bit less brutality. That part he never let us forget. "You should just be glad you didn't have it as bad as I did," he'd say.

My dad learned from his father that life was hard, and he believed beating his kids would prepare us for that. He also felt strongly he needed to keep us out of trouble. His fear of trouble was well founded. It stemmed from his time as a boy living in Chicago, where he feared the mafia, and then later his time spent in the Air Force in the aftermath of World War II. Although he never saw combat—he used his electrical expertise to teach communications—he told us how in the military, his own side would just as soon kill him because he was Jewish.

As such, he expected us to "keep our noses clean" and never volunteer the information that we were Jewish. Although we didn't hide our heritage, we didn't openly display it either. We knew it could cause problems down the line.

This was life living under Dad's roof—stay out of trouble and if you don't, expect a beating; not necessarily out of rage, but to teach a lesson. The abuse, however, emotionally scarred us just the same.

My mother, Norma, was something of a counterbalance to Dad's rigidity. Beautiful and vivacious, she had dark brown eyes and thick, wavy chestnut brown hair that she cherished. She represented that more spiritual side of the family's heritage. An extremely artistic and intelligent woman, Mom tried to protect us—she still beat us, but she also protected us. She was also the source of any money her children saw. While my dad made the money and wouldn't spend it, my mom largely controlled it. If we were ever in need of money, we'd come to her. She mostly adhered to my dad's frugal mentality, but she would sneak my brothers and me something from time to time.

Her own upbringing wasn't that different from Dad's. Her mother was sent here with her sister when she was sixteen from Ukraine. Their family was supposed to follow. However, after the sisters received a couple of letters, they never heard from their family again.

My mother's mother, whom we called Bubbe (Yiddish for grandmother), married very young and had my mom when she was still a teen. Her husband left, and my mom was thrust into a role of responsibility from then on. She did everything for my grandmother, including reading and writing for her. However, that didn't save her from being beaten by Bubbe. My grandmother beat my mother so badly that my mom moved out and lived with another relative for many years.

Just like my dad, my mom modeled her parenting on her own experiences, whether she intended to or not. Mom used to tell us, "If you don't like something, you can leave!" "How?" I'd say, thinking *how am I supposed to leave when I am just a child?* "You make arrangements," she'd say simply, with a shrug. That is what she had done.

Like Dad, Mom also viewed herself as restrained compared to what she had endured. She told me a story about a fire truck passing her school as a child. She wanted to know where it was going, so she followed it, but in doing so, she arrived home later than usual. As punishment, her mother tied her to the porch for the entire night. "At least I've never tied you to the porch," she'd say.

But focusing only on the abuse is unfair to her. Mom was also the family's moral compass. She was small at only just five feet tall, but she was a fighter. She made arrangements to leave home at eight and moved out at twelve. True to the wisdom of her great-great-father-in-law, she was a principled "fight for change" type of person, and she instilled in me that you fight for everyone's rights and educate everyone you can. She'd stand up to the police in the 1960s in Los Angeles, despite the risks of being beaten.

Mom was bold and unafraid to act on what she believed in. When she first met my dad, she asked him out, declaring he was the man she was going to marry. She was also a voracious reader who could write in Yiddish.

Still, my mom faced struggles, too. She battled depression and would lock herself in her room for a week at a time. She also held terrible grudges. If she was mad at me, she'd tell me not to speak to her for ten days. She felt changes in the weather, and the onset of rain would bring about a migraine.

For all her struggles, at her core, her priority was her family. My brothers and I would encourage her to divorce Dad, although she always refused. She couldn't raise all four of us on her own, she'd say, and besides, someday, *we'd* protect *her*.

I never saw my dad raise a hand to my mom, but horrible arguments ensued between the two of them behind closed doors. Often, they'd end with my mom depressed, retreating to her room sometimes for a week or more.

VIOLENT HOME

The violence and abuse in my home went beyond occasional spankings. My father never hugged me. Nor did he ever tell me he loved me.

The reason was simple. Not only was he insecure about money, he was insecure about himself. Dad would try to hold us back. My brothers and I often talked about what we'd do if something ever happened to Mom. We predicted Dad would be in his workshop every night, leaving us to fend for ourselves. As kids, that scared us. Dad was so into his own life and work that it seemed he was completely uninterested in us—and whatever interest he had was violent.

Top row: Martin holding Ross, (bottom L-R) Mark and Paul

Unfortunately, my parents shared that interest. Throughout our childhood, my mother would spank my brothers and me. To protect ourselves, we would place 78 rpm records or pie pans in our pants. This made our mother laugh, though the spankings continued. It happened so often that we learned to walk around with our butt muscles tightened so she'd hurt her wrist if she hit us. So engrained was this behavior, I did it until I was in my mid-twenties.

When Mom couldn't handle doling out the abuse herself, she would have my dad do it. Dad would come home from a long day of work and hit us, without even knowing why. He'd take off his leather belt—he called it "the strap"—fold it in his hand, hold the buckle, and whip us until he left welts. I remember my brothers and I counting each other's welts in our rooms afterward, running our fingers gently over each one so we knew where they were since we didn't have a mirror.

If we really misbehaved, Dad would make us take off all of our clothes until we were naked and hit us. Then he threw us—still naked—into the front yard and locked the door.

That wasn't the only time my parents locked us out.

Around the time I was ten, Paul and I shared a room. If we kept messing around after our parents told us to go to sleep, they would throw us outside, lock the door, and tell us to sleep out there. You can imagine how scary this was for a snot-nosed kid plagued by nightmares. It was all the worse because we lived at the end of a street. There were no lights on, no neighbors with TVs blinking in the window. Locked out, we felt completely isolated and exposed. And we couldn't get to the two people meant to protect us.

Luckily, my parents left the car unlocked, so we could crawl in there and sleep. In the morning, the door to the house would be unlocked.

Instances like this weren't particularly frequent, but they happened often enough.

It's worth saying that this was not considered excessive for the times. In those days, my parents weren't the only ones treating their kids this way. If somebody happened to walk by while we were in the front yard, locked out as punishment, they'd probably just say, "The Kenzer boys are in trouble again."

No one saw it as abusive. My parents thought they were holding back, even. In my father's eyes, he was morphing us from the animals we were as kids into the human beings we'd become as adults. In his mind, he was giving us what we needed—a lesson from the school of hard knocks. It would be many years before either of my parents could see how wrong they were.

And we did have some sources of love in our lives. My father's younger brother Jules, by far the most spiritual of that family, used to come and love on us, especially Paul and me. We were always excited when Jules would come for a visit because he would spend quality time with us—holding us, listening to our stories, and telling us that he loved us and that we could do great things. I can remember Jules yelling at my father in the next room about how my father was damaging us and how we were going to grow up to hate him.

Jules was right in a lot of ways. We did grow to hate my father. It was a hate that grew out of hurt love—a love that I would find could endure anything—but it was hate all the same.

If this was my whole story, you could expect a book about an average boy growing up the way many such boys did in the '50s and '60s. But while much of this reality lined up with difficult childhoods for others from my generation, there was something more going on in my family. Those nightmares weren't a fluke. They were one of many signs that there was a deeper, spiritual understanding in certain members of the family.

THE VALUE OF MEDITATION

Much of the meaning behind the suffering I experienced in childhood was revealed to me through meditation.

I wasn't born aware of meditation, of course. My lack of understanding made those early years all the harder to bear. It wasn't until I read the *Autobiography of a Yogi*, an event I will recount ahead, that I set out to learn to meditate. It wasn't easy. In the beginning, I would fall asleep within the first five minutes. But I persevered, and soon I was meditating twenty minutes a day. Then thirty minutes twice a day. Eventually, I was meditating for an hour both morning and evening.

Meditation is a form of prayer, and prayer is a form of meditation. Chanting is also a form of meditation. However, there are differences. Meditation, unlike prayer, is not about asking for something; it is about going deep in one's consciousness and listening.

One may begin to hear "om," the cosmic vibration that supports all of creation. Soon after, this vibration becomes a loving conversation—usually with God, and many times with other yogis who are also in deep meditation. Visions sometimes arise as well. Mundane visions should be ignored in the same way that we ignore the chattering of the mind, but other visions are more worthy of attention and remembrance. In deeper awareness, one may see cosmic lights and perhaps the Milky Way or other universes.

Regardless of what visuals arise, one will obtain a deep sense of peace and well-being.

There is no limit to where one can go, but the goal is not to get too identified with any type of distraction. I have seen my chakras, even my Crown Chakra, many times. So many times, in fact, that I am no longer interested in running after these types of experiences. If they come, they come.

This is most likely due to the fact that I have practiced meditation in previous lifetimes. In the same way that if you were attracted to this book enough to pick it up and read it, we have something in common. We are all on this journey together.

CHAPTER 2

A FAMILY IN TWO WORLDS

LOOKING BACK, MY CHILDHOOD WAS DEFINED IN CONtrasts—secular and spiritual beliefs; protection and abuse; ordinary and extraordinary—all juxtaposed in a family wrought by our past.

Of my two parents, my mom brought the spiritual element to our family. Myself and my younger brother, Ross, inherited mom's spirituality, along with her same sensitivities. Ross, I often say, lived in a *Wizard of Oz* kind of world. He was extremely sensitive—if he witnessed any of his brothers fighting, he would cry. While it wasn't diagnosed back then, I now believe Ross was on the ADHD spectrum or had a learning disability. He was also gay, and it was much harder to be homosexual in those times. Overall, he just saw things differently than most, and that really defined his life in many ways.

While both Ross and I took after our mother in having more direct connection to the spiritual world, we all dealt and struggled with it differently. Mom largely ignored this connection. While she was never shocked to hear what I was experiencing and clearly had similar experiences herself, she simply didn't allow it to touch her life.

"Weren't you ever religious or spiritual?" I once asked her. "Weren't you ever interested in God?"

At the very mention of the idea, her face lit up. "As a matter of fact, yes," she confided. During her adolescence, she would come home from school and read the Bible everyday.

"What happened?" I asked.

"I met your father," she said bluntly. "He told me I was wasting my time."

For many years of my life, I adopted that same perspective—having little, and at times no, interest in my spiritual life. In fact, I mistook my psychic awareness for spiritual cultivation. Only after all the Self-Realization and awakening I will tell you about in this book did I see how my direct connection could strengthen me. I can't say the same for Ross, whose spirituality and sensitivity may have been what led to his early death.

Meanwhile, my dad, while secularly Jewish, was not a spiritual man. Dad cared about being Jewish as an identity (one we should strictly be careful about revealing), not a religious belief system, and that's what he taught us to do, too. He would seek out other Jewish people, or proudly inform us a comedian or celebrity was Jewish. We were raised to be part of the Jewish community, but we didn't actually practice the religion. Overall, in the battle between my father's secular Jewishness and my mother's spiritual beliefs, the secular won out.

My two older brothers, Martin and Paul, fell in line with Dad's beliefs. Martin has always seen the spiritual as nonsense. Paul, for a time, fell somewhere in between the two options. Although early on he was quite receptive to the spiritual, today he says he agrees with Dad and Martin's thinking.

FALLING OUTSIDE THE STANDARD CATEGORIES

None of us could deny, though, that some extremely unique events happened to us growing up.

For example, every night our family would gather around the dinner table to eat—a completely ordinary thing for a family to do. However, for a time, every evening, we heard someone pounding on the outside of the kitchen wall. The pounding was not coming from the backyard. It appeared to be coming from inside the wall.

The noise was unexplainable. We'd look out to see if someone was there but saw no one. And anyway, we had dogs who would bark if someone had been there. This went on for quite some time. Every evening during dinner, that knocking returned.

One night, I walked into the kitchen and found my mom seemingly talking to a person who wasn't there.

"You're welcome to stay here; I don't care if you're here," she said. "But the knocking is going to have to stop if you're going to stay."

She said it so matter of factly. I was shocked. I had no idea my mom knew about talking to entities, but watching her have that conversation, it was clear she had some spiritual connection.

We never heard the knocking again.

Other occurrences bolstered my belief in our connection with the spiritual world and God. One such example happened when I was nine and I decided I couldn't take my nightmares anymore.

As part of our Jewish identity, my parents sent my brothers and me to Hebrew School to study the Bible, but none of us took to it. We believed in God, in theory, but I didn't really know what that meant.

Still, I was desperate and exhausted. So one night, for the first time ever, I prayed to God. I spoke ten magic words:

"Please God, don't let me have any more bad dreams."

It worked. The first night, I didn't have a bad dream. The second night, I didn't have a bad dream.

I told my mother, "Do you know why I didn't have any bad dreams? It's because I started praying."

She told me she didn't have a problem with my praying. Still, perhaps due to the influence of my mistrustful father, I swore her to secrecy. It seemed like something that should not be revealed.

These early experiences signaled a strong association to the Divine in my house, but I also realized at a young age that not everyone had these connections. At school, no one else had a mother who told ghosts to stop knocking on the wall at dinner time. No one else had a brother who saw a moon rise from behind his dresser. And no one else had inescapable nightmarish visions of their past lives every night.

But it was something more banal that drove this point home for me. In first grade, kids would ask me if I believed in Santa and God. I mentioned this to my mother, who told me point-blank: God is real, Santa is not. But, she cautioned, don't tell the other kids about Santa. Their parents want them to believe.

I registered the strangeness of this understanding. God was real, Santa was not, but I couldn't disabuse kids of the difference. I had a hidden knowledge of the way the universe worked, but I was bound to keep it to myself.

This was only the start of my frustrations. When I asked Mom where God was, she couldn't tell me. "I don't know," she said. "The heavens?"

"Where's that?" I asked, and she just looked up at the sky.

I think back to this conversation often because it's perfectly representative of my childhood as I navigated life at the border of my spiritual and physical worlds. I *knew* there was something more to me—and my family—that didn't fit with the standard, but I couldn't comprehend it. Neither could my mom—or anyone in our household for that matter.

But I longed to understand, and much of my childhood would be spent exploring the unexplainable.

FINDING THE LIMITS OF DIRECT CONNECTION

Even something as simple as checking out a book at the library pointed back to my connection with the spiritual world and a yearning for knowledge. When I was eight, my dad took me to get my library card. As the librarian showed me the children's section, she asked what I wanted to read about.

"ESP," I said. The librarian couldn't believe it, but all this child in front of her wanted to read about was extrasensory perception.

I most certainly wouldn't find anything on that here, she told me, but I was free to check out books from the adult section. I came home that day with a stack of books about ESP. They were probably way beyond my reading level, but I was determined to learn.

This exploration of the spiritual was my whole life as a child.

I tried, unsuccessfully, to walk through walls and move objects with my mind. I practiced predicting cards—not the way magicians do it as a trick, but through psychic force. When I let go and stopped trying so hard, I could do it (though not when attention was focused upon me).

Once, I was practicing my card prediction with Paul when our father entered the room and asked what we were doing. "Reading cards," I replied, shuffling the deck. Then I turned the top card to face my father while saying "three of Clubs." The next was a Queen of Hearts. Then a Jack of Spades, and lastly a six of Spades. My father's eyes grew large. "You got all of them correct! You've got something here. Do some more." But when I felt the attention and pressure on me, I was unable to accurately continue.

Successfully or not, I was always testing the boundaries of my connection in an attempt to understand it.

One source for learning was animals. I picked up early on that if you pay attention to these creatures, they'll teach you a lot. I've continued to do that throughout my life.

At one point, my family owned four dogs, and each son was responsible for one. My dog's name was Rajah.

Now, while I was experiencing some amazing spiritual realities as a child, it's important to know that I was also extremely depressed. I'd go to school sick and tired, having not slept because of my dreams and my health, only to feel like I didn't quite belong. After all, I was keeping secrets from the other kids. I perceived myself as different. Then, I'd trudge home, never knowing what the night would hold for me—a "lesson" from my parents? A night spent out in the car? A terrifying dream?

Sometimes, it was all of it. The weight of these difficulties left me at times feeling suicidal.

But when I came home to Rajah, he'd lick my face. If I tried to push him away, he would back up and sit on me. If I tried to get up, he'd gently nip at my hands. He didn't want me to move; he just wanted me to be still with him. It was like he knew everything I felt internally.

Paul's dog, Venus, a German Shepherd, gave me similar affection. When I'd lay out in the sun on our driveway, Venus would lie on top of me and place her face up against mine. After a moment, she'd go off and run, but it was her sweet way of letting me know she was there for me.

These stories of Rajah and Venus aren't anything out of the

ordinary. Dogs every day show their owners unconditional love. But for me, these were my only real lessons of physical love and intimacy. I believe these dogs recognized that's what I—a sick, abused, tormented kid—needed. And I wasn't going to get it anywhere else.

There also were more obvious signs that our pets, just like our family, straddled the line between normal and extraordinary.

Ross's dog, Georgie, a poodle, had the ability to heal. When any of us boys had a scab or a wound, Georgie would come to our aid. Sometimes, he would insist on opening the scab and cleaning it out. When he sensed that it was healing properly on its own, he left it alone to heal.

Martin's dog, Foxie, the mother of Rajah and Venus, had a way about her that indicated to me that she may have been a human in a previous life. Foxie refused to be captive. She would escape over the fence with Rajah and go on these incredible journeys. It would take days for Rajah to find his way home—if a person approached him, he would run away, never trusting them. Foxie, on the other hand, would go right up to the person and let them read her tag. Then, she'd let the person give her a ride home.

When she was home, Foxie would jump on a chair at the table and expect dinner. Beyond these behavioral indications, Foxie seemed to understand everything we did—perhaps because, at one point, she had been just like us.

For me, my relationships with these dogs further uncovered how my connection extended beyond my own thoughts and dreams. While much of what they did was standard dog stuff, there were extraordinary things about them that indicated more going on. And I, having this direct connection, was very tuned in.

PREDICTING THE FUTURE

As I grew older, my relationship with the spiritual world strengthened. Along with this strengthening, I became aware of lower and higher material realms, and my psychic abilities increased. I began seeing future events unfolding in my dreams.

The first time this happened, I was lying in bed in a semi-trance state—the sort when you aren't quite awake but you aren't asleep either. At that moment, I heard the doorbell. It was my aunt and uncle, Fran and Sid, and I could smell they brought fresh bagels. I couldn't quite make out the muffled conversation through the walls—not that I cared about what the adults had to say anyhow. But I finally got up to join them.

When I walked into the kitchen, however, it was only my mother. Sitting there, drinking coffee.

Puzzled, I asked, "Where are Fran and Sid?"

"What are you talking about?" Mom responded. She seemed equally confused but didn't care enough to actually look up from her coffee and newspaper.

"They were here," I insisted. "Didn't you just have bagels?"

"Mark, I don't know what you're talking about," my mom replied. "It's just me."

But that night, Fran and Sid did come over. And they brought bagels. My mother gave me a look. Nothing more needed to be said.

This sort of thing started happening more and more often. I spent a lot of time sitting alone in our family's den and staring off into nothing. When I did this, I discovered I could project forward in time.

The sensation of projecting was nothing like I'd ever felt. Everything shut down and turned within. I still had awareness, but anything I did, I did perfectly. I could sit and play the piano without a single mistake. Whatever I was thinking, it was pure thinking. This is like being "in the zone" in sports. In such moments, focus becomes internalized as most outside awareness is turned inward.

I didn't know it then, but I was experiencing a samadhi—a state of oneness in which you withdraw energy from your senses and direct it between you and God, touching the Divine. Most of us get this feeling at one time or another—this one-pointedness where all of our energy is focused, but I got it all the time as a kid. I started to hear "om"—the sound vibration of God—whenever I entered this state. I didn't know what the sound was then, only that whenever I projected, I would hear it.

With my awareness growing, I began to attempt astral projection when I went to bed. I would put a dime or quarter in my underwear (in case I ended up somewhere and needed to call to get home) and imagined myself in India. It was always India, although I didn't understand why at the time.

While I was there, I saw myself picking up objects to bring back home. I was also very fascinated in these visions with swamis and fakirs, Hindu and Muslim religous devotees. From this, I knew my future would involve mysticism and importing mystical objects from that part of the world. India, in fact, would have a profound impact on the rest of my life.

For much of my childhood, spiritual experiences and an unexplainable connection to God consumed my life. I was aware of it and sensitive to it, but I didn't quite understand it. I would spend hours trying to do so, all against the backdrop of the abuse and suffering I endured.

As I grew, my life would continue to intersect the spiritual world and the material one. What I would come to find out is that often great progress in my spiritual understanding would be accompanied by a period in which the material world would really fight back.

EXPLAINING OUR ATTRACTION
TO SPIRITUAL IDEAS

Even as a child, I found myself strangely attracted to spiritual ideas and practices that I really knew little about, like the Hare Krishnas. And no wonder. I was simply more sensitive to certain opulences than most. Vedic wisdom teaches us that our attractions are driven by six opulences:

- Renunciation
- Beauty
- Strength
- Fame
- Wealth
- Knowledge

As people, we may express certain opulences in large amounts, and we are drawn to those who exemplify various opulences. This is why people are so interested in celebrities, athletes, politicians, and brilliant minds. However, we must remember that none of these opulences exist in the material world in perfection. There is always someone who is richer, smarter, or more famous.

When we turn these six opulences to the spiritual world, it helps explain our attractions to varying religions, even when we have roots just in one. All religions aim to express—sometimes imperfectly—our relationship to the one entity to contain all six opulences: God.

God has all six in full. S/He is the Most Attractive, the Most

Powerful, the Most Intelligent, the Most Renounced, the Wealthiest and of course, the Most Famous.

I remember my friend Todd once telling me about meeting a Holy Man. "Mark," Todd said enthusiastically, "he had no pockets!" Not understanding the point, I asked Todd what that meant to him. "He doesn't have any keys. He doesn't own anything. He's free!" Todd was obviously attracted to the opulence of renunciation, as were the people of Jesus's and Gandhi's time.

Throughout my life, I have gained wisdom from Jewish, Christian, Muslim, Hindu, Buddhist, and many other practices. Rarely has a single text or concept ever presented the entire truth, but none have entirely missed it either. Tibetan Buddhism, for example, revealed my childhood dreams were bardo states; the samadhi states I experienced when projecting forward in time are rooted in Hindu and Buddhist beliefs; and the visions of swamis and fakirs that dominated my astral projections point to Hindu and Muslim ideologies. And Jesus was the first spirit to act in my life and guide me toward deeper knowledge.

The ideas in this book are not in conflict with the true nature of any religion because all religions point us in one direction—that of the Self and God Realization.

CHAPTER 3

MEETING THE SAINTS

INTO MY EARLY TEENS, I CONTINUED TO EXPLORE LIFE IN my dual worlds. Spiritually, I experimented with skills like astral projection, although these practices didn't consume my life like they once had. Instead, I started spending more time with people who interested me.

One such person was a girl named Pat. I met Pat through her brother, Bob Davis, who would grow up to be the punk rock pioneer Chuck Wagon in the band, The Dickies. Bob and I had started walking to high school together and struck up a friendship. For a while, Bob and I even played together in a garage rock band.

Bob was my friend, but Pat fascinated me. Pat didn't put any effort into being attractive—choosing jeans and a t-shirt over a dress and makeup—but she was all the same. Dark-haired and quick to smile, she was older than us, about twenty-one at the time—and extremely smart and artistic. She got me one of my first jobs at a place called Pizza Man, a pizza delivery restaurant. During work, we'd sit around and talk whenever we had the chance, and after shifts, Pat would give me a ride home. After a time, our relationship became sexual.

One day, I decided to try astral projection while I was wide awake. I was finding it increasingly difficult to project at night because I'd fall asleep and forget what happened. So early one morning, while still in bed, I entered my trance state. I dressed and put on a jacket, and I decided to go see Pat. I walked the whole fifteen minutes to her house, even stopping at a red light along the way—I wasn't sure if I could be hit by a car in this state. When I got there, I rang the doorbell. The door opened, and I floated into the house on a pile of white smoke.

I walked into Pat's room and woke her up. She looked at me, groggily, still half asleep and confused.

"Pat, this is Mark," I said gently, putting my hand on her shoulder. "I want you to get up. I need you to talk to me."

She still wasn't fully awake. I looked over at the clock and saw it was twenty to eight. When she finally came to, I said, "I want you to call me at eight o'clock."

Pat looked at me, then put her head back down and closed her eyes.

"Pat, you're going to call me at eight o'clock, right? You're going to remember?" I urged.

"Yes, Mark, I'll remember," she said tiredly, shooing me away and burying her face back into her pillow.

I walked all the way home. Cars passed me on Van Nuys Boulevard as the city began to wake up. I reached my house, went back to my room, and took off my clothes. As I laid my body down, I felt the weight of my spirit push me into the bed. It scared me a bit—I realized I really had been gone. As I was processing that, the phone rang.

I knew who it was before I picked it up.

"Pat," I answered. "Why are you calling me?"

"Why shouldn't I call you?" she replied on the other end of the line, still sounding confused.

I told Pat what happened: I had astral projected to her and prompted her to call me at eight o'clock—and it worked.

My heart raced. I felt overwhelmed with emotions. The memories from my journey were so vivid.

I hung up and ran to tell my parents. Then, the phone rang again. It was Pat. Her dad told her that someone had rung the doorbell that morning but when he'd answered, no one was there.

If I needed any further proof of my abilities, I certainly had it now.

DO YOU STILL LOVE ME?

Despite this new evidence, after my experience at Pat's, I found myself continuing to pull away from these practices. Spiritually, I knew what I was capable of, and as a fifteen-year-old boy in the midst of puberty, my other interests in Pat were far more enticing than astral projection.

This stronger tug from the material side wasn't all sexual, and it had actually begun even before my teen years. Major changes in my life had already started drawing my attention away from the spiritual world.

When I was about twelve, my mother picked me up from school. We were sitting in the car together and talking. For all our trouble, she was something of my best friend growing up. She once told me that she wished she had a daughter because it was hard to raise four boys and have no one to talk to. So I tried to fill that role for her.

When she took up painting, I'd go and watch her paint. In her studio, I would watch her do the most wonderful things with color. "Mark, watch," she said once, drawing me close to her pallet. "I take a bit of this," she said, picking up some paint from the chaos of colors on the board. "If I want to draw out the yellow from it, then I warm it up by adding a little of this."

In front of my eyes, the mystery of light and color took me for a ride. The color slowly changed, not in the ordinary way that we had learned in elementary school by blending two primary colors together, but by the percentages of hues changing in the world right before us. In the same way a green bell pepper will turn to red and then orange, so my mom transformed one shade into another. To me, it was magic.

Once I got past the age of playing childhood games, I often chose spending time with Mom over friends. When I was bored or frustrated, I'd go to her and we'd talk.

Doing this, I heard all about how my mother's life wasn't working. My father was extremely dismissive of her interests, her family, and her experiences. While Mom clearly had spiritual sensitivities, it didn't seem to bring her the same comfort that it had and would come to bring me. In this way, I realized how lost Mom was as a person.

Because of our closeness, however, that day in the car, I felt I could ask her a big question that had been weighing heavily on my mind: "Do you not love me anymore?"

She looked crestfallen. "Why would you say that, Mark?"

"You don't hit us anymore," I said.

She shook her head mournfully. "I realized I was sick," she explained. She had put herself through therapy and discovered how wrong she'd been to beat my brothers and me.

"Why doesn't Dad do it anymore?" I asked.

"Because I told him to stop," she answered.

I was shocked. I had to realign things in my mind. I had always associated being hit with getting attention because for so long that was the main way I received it from my parents. When each of our dogs died, my mom held me as I cried, but those were exceptional instances, not the norm.

It was a bittersweet moment for me. After years of being abused, it had finally come to an end. But the emotional damage had already been done. Talk about a double-edged sword.

I had a very different but somewhat related moment with my father later. My most lasting and deepest memories as a child up until the age of twelve were the constant beatings that I received not just from my parents but the torture inflicted upon me by my oldest brother Martin (seven years my senior). I thought that this was the norm in every family, and I, too, would inflict pain into the life of my brother Ross, who was three years younger than me.

As I grew older and stronger, though, I began to seek out my moment to fight back against my older sibling, and even my father, and to beat the hell out of them for all the pain they'd caused me. I began taking martial arts lessons, and after some time, I finally seemed to get my chance to show my strength when Martin put me in a headlock.

But that fight was never meant to be because my father walked into the room and did the most surprising thing. He shouted at Martin and threatened him. "If I ever see you touching Mark again in any way, I'll kick you out of this house!" he yelled.

This was a man who frequently told my brothers and me— either directly or indirectly—that we were worthless. I don't recall him ever telling me that I was good, or that I had done well. When I got older and consciously attempted to seek his approval, he would avoid me. When I confronted him, he would leave the room if I persisted. And yet here he was, defending me—protecting me. Though it came through a form of violence, I knew on some level, it was love.

NEW HEALTH

There were other profound changes in my life at this stage, particularly to my health.

My headaches and migraines continued into late childhood, and I still had sinus problems. Living in Los Angeles's famously lead-filled smoggy air, I just never felt healthy.

That started to change when we went on our first-ever family vacation to Hawaii. I was thirteen, and the trip was amazing for my health. The islands, I noticed, were so clean and primitive. There was no smog or pollution to be found. Not once did I get a headache or a migraine. For the first time in my life, I didn't feel sick at all.

After we returned, I decided to explore ways to take back my health. I discovered that the sinus issues I had long battled were due to a milk allergy—my parents had continued to give it to me, but I couldn't digest it. Eliminating milk from my diet resolved those issues almost immediately.

Then, a few years later, I started juicing. It was an idea I credit my brother Paul's friend, Todd, with providing me. Todd was on his own spiritual journey and would eventually become a member of the Brothers of the Wind, also known as Christ's Family, for a short time. But his out-there perspective was what I needed to finally own my health.

Todd suggested that juicing fruits and vegetables would relieve my ailments. He also pushed me toward vegetarianism. When I adopted these habits, I started to feel remarkably healthier. The headaches and migraines decreased—even in LA. At last, my battle with chronic sickness was over, at least for now.

For the first time ever, I felt like I was living a somewhat normal life, although I was never fully normal as most would define it. I still had this distinctive connection to the spiritual world that impacted me even when I didn't expect it.

Healthier and free of abuse, you might assume I now had time to concentrate on my studies. You'd be wrong. My formal education during my high school years was mostly based on learning how best to cut class—but my spiritual education thrived. This was largely because saints and spiritual ideas continued to make their way into my everyday life, whether I sought them out or not.

One day, for example, Pat took Bob and me to a bookstore and showed me a picture of her grandmother's guru, Paramahansa Yogananda, on the cover of *Autobiography of a Yogi*. I noted how unusual it was for Pat's grandmother to even *have* a guru, given that her family was conservative Christian.

"You might want to read it," urged Pat.

I shrugged. The book looked interesting. I thought the guru kind of looked like my grandmother. But I set it back down.

I didn't know it at the time, but instances like this were planting seeds for me to come back to and explore later. Years after this, I would read *Autobiography of a Yogi* and finish it, cover to cover, in just a few days. And it would change my life forever.

Around the same time, Paul had a book called *Krsna: The Supreme Personality of Godhead* by A.C. Bhaktivedanta Swami, also known as Prabhupada to his disciples.

I flipped through it. "You're reading this?" I asked, surprised.

I stopped on a page with a picture I didn't understand. It was an image of Krishna, with blue-colored skin.

"Do you think God is blue?"

Paul shrugged. "That's what the book says."

Puzzled, I once again put the book down. The conversation ended there, but another seed was planted.

Books, in fact, would always play a large role in my spiritual learning. Growing up Jewish, books were sacred, and I read almost every single one on my parents' shelves. It was an eclectic collection, ranging from psychology publications to novels and my mom's spiritual and therapy books.

I wasn't the only one in my family who constantly read. My oldest brother, Martin, was so outwardly intelligent that he would read pretty much anything he could get his hands on to quench his thirst for knowledge. That may be how he came to share a book with me by Herman Hesse called *Siddartha*. It was about the life of the Buddha.

"You should read this," Martin said, handing me the book. "I think you'll like it."

It was certainly an uncharacteristic choice for Martin, but I took his word for it, and he was right. I couldn't put it down, although I didn't know why. It was another instance of being drawn to the spiritual side, even without my conscious effort to do so.

There were other spiritual experiences that continued to pepper my teenage life, as well. On our birthdays, for example, our parents would take my brothers and me out to a restaurant or activity of our choice. I always chose Chinatown because I had a deep interest in the East.

On one particular birthday in Chinatown, the Hare Krishnas were on the street, and I was fascinated and supremely attracted to the whole scene. The robes they wore, the renunciation, the incense they gave out, it all pulled me in a way I didn't even understand. Later, I would come to be turned off by the movement after Prabhupada left his body, but at the time, I felt drawn to connect to it, despite, again, not really knowing why.

THE MATERIAL WORLD STRIKES BACK

While my spiritual understanding and exposures generally grew in my teenage years without conflicting with my interests in girls and music, there were times when my Divine connection and mortal existence collided head on. Two such instances happened around the age of sixteen.

The first event started with a vision. I was still spending time in the den, projecting into the future, when I saw something major was about to happen to our family.

I saw a fire. It was at our rental property—a house next door that my parents owned. My mom had turned the property into an artist's studio so she could paint undisturbed. I had converted the kitchen into a dark room for a photography class I was taking.

When I told my parents what I saw, my father dismissed it. "If anyone is going to burn our house down, it's going to be you," he said, referring to my photography lights.

Yet, some time later, a neighbor ran up to our house. "Your field is on fire!" he yelled.

There was a bamboo field behind our second house. Some kids were playing with matches, and they lit the bamboo on fire. I ran over to try to put it out and some neighbors joined in. Finally, the fire department arrived and put it all out. From then on, my family took my visions a bit more seriously.

About six months later, my projections alerted me to another big event—I saw my dad getting arrested.

My dad collected antique slot machines. At the time, all gaming devices—including slot machines—were illegal. The law considered them contraband; my father, on the other hand, viewed them as fine Americana works of art.

After foreseeing his arrest, I warned my father that he should stop dealing with slot machines. At first, he once again dismissed my suggestion—this hobby was something he loved. But my mom urged him to reconsider.

"You should listen to him," she said. "He was right about the fire."

He couldn't argue that, he admitted. But he couldn't help himself. He had just one last machine he had committed to selling. He would see that through and then stop. I told him to stop *now*. Don't do that last sale. But he didn't listen. The buyer, he said, was coming all the way from another county.

The next morning, I heard a pounding at the front door. It was 7 a.m., the time my dad's buyer was to arrive and buy the slot machine. But when I answered the door, I learned the truth—the man my dad thought he was selling to was an undercover police officer.

"Your father is under arrest and handcuffed next door," he said. "We're coming in."

Instinctively, I refused, blocking the door from opening further with my foot. "You can't come in here!" I shouted.

"Why not?" the plain-clothes officer replied.

I didn't know that I had an answer. I was as surprised as him when I informed the officer that we had dogs in the house. I then closed the door, woke my mother, and locked the dogs in the kitchen, knowing that the police would have to go past the dogs to get to the three slot machines in the den, which could only be accessed through the dog-filled kitchen. They might hurt the dogs if I didn't keep them away.

My mother and I then let the large brute into our home. He immediately tried to remove a number of dice machines that were on display in our living room. Again, out of nowhere I blurted out, "You can't take those!"

I didn't know why not, but the words followed. "There is no place to put a coin, they are not for gambling."

With that, they left the machines alone.

I went next door to check on my handcuffed father. He also

looked like he'd been roughed up by the police standing over him. He told me to get my camera and take photos of everything. I documented the scene as a big van came and took all the slot machines away, save for the one in the den, which I convinced them wasn't actually a slot machine because it didn't have a coin slot.

Afterward, my family spent the rest of the day bailing my dad out of jail. Then, a bit of a media frenzy ensued. Helicopters flew over our house; we were followed in our cars; we were interviewed by the news. We hired an attorney—at great expense—to defend my dad and get his collection back.

And believe it or not, my dad won the case. In fact, my father's case set a precedent that would change the law across the country. Within a few years, the collecting of antique gambling machines became legal throughout the US.

When it was all said and done, our family went to pick up Dad's machines. One was missing, as well as a set of lock picks made by the man who made Harry Houdini's lock picks. Apparently, they were stolen by the police.

This wouldn't be my last run-in with the law or the courts, although as I got older, I wouldn't always take the time to predict it would happen. In fact, the events that followed would suspend the progress of my spiritual trajectory for years and cause me immense pain before I would find my way back again.

JOE, JEFF, JERRY...JAIL

It was when I was around twenty years old that the realities of material life really came crashing down.

It all started with a friend—Jeff Jampol. Jeff and I had been close since childhood. Growing up, we seemed to live parallel lives. We were both the third son in families with four boys.

We both had fathers from Chicago. We both got hit at home. Later, that parallel would extend to losing our younger brothers at an early age.

We were also both tall, Jewish, and intelligent, and we had similar tastes. We shared a love of rock music—like my other friend, Bob Davis, Jeff would go on to make a career out of that. He now manages dead rock stars, including The Doors, Michael Jackson, Janis Joplin, and others. Jeff was a lively, charismatic character, but he also had his demons—he'd eventually become addicted to heroin.

Jeff had a cousin, Jerry, who was two years older than I was. Jerry was my brother Paul's classmate. We had met at Paul's tenth birthday party. One night, in our late teens, I was hanging out with Jeff when he mentioned he'd gotten a job at Ten Little Indians, a jewelry company Jerry worked at. He thought I might be interested in getting a job there, too.

I soon learned that Jerry wanted to start his own, similar company, and had plans to do so with another cousin, Jamie. But Jamie didn't like working with Jerry very much, and after meeting me, Jamie suggested I go into business with him instead. So Jamie and I opened our own place in Los Angeles on Sunset Boulevard. It was called The Chain Reaction.

The business model for The Chain Reaction was similar to Ten Little Indians: we sold cheap jewelry for a large profit. Our inventory included sterling silver, costume Indian jewelry, and 12-karat gold-filled jewelry (gold filled means it's gold on the outside but filled with a less expensive material on the inside).

Shortly after opening The Chain Reaction with Jamie, I decided I could do this same sort of business on my own. I met a potential partner, Joe, also through my brother Paul, who was seeking a career change. He joined me in opening a separate business in Santa Clara. We called it The Chain Gang, and it followed the same business model as The Chain Reaction. Everything for The Chain Gang was in Joe's name. I ran things as a silent partner.

At first, it seemed I'd made a wise choice. The Chain Reaction didn't do well, but The Chain Gang was quite successful. We'd sell any piece of jewelry for twenty dollars and give a second piece for free. Each piece came with a lifetime guarantee. It only cost us three dollars to produce a pair, so we ran at a healthy profit.

To sell this jewelry, we advertised for salespeople to go door to door. We brought in Jeff, who was still working for Ten Little Indians, to hire, train, and manage the new team. His big, colorful personality was perfect for the role.

With salespeople on board and management in place, The Chain Gang began making us loads of money. I was living with my girlfriend, Sandy, who ran the front desk at our office. Unlike Pat, Sandy was conscious of her attractiveness. She wore her hair down her back because it accentuated her looks and the many dresses she wore. But she was not vain or unserious. She had a professional air about her, and a sweet, warm smile. With her at my side and the business growing, everything seemed to be going well.

Then one night, Sandy came home worried.

"Mark, you need to be concerned about this," she said. "The TV news called us. Something's wrong."

The next day when I went to work, I learned something was, in fact, very wrong. The parking lot was filled with police cars. I walked into the office to see Jeff in handcuffs and Joe sweating bullets.

"They're all arrested," Joe said, referring to Jeff and the other salespeople in the office. "They're still deciding what to do with me." I looked around. Everything from our office was being confiscated.

As it turned out, two of our salesmen had gone to a jeweler in Monterey and tried to sell our jewelry as real gold. This went against everything we stood for as a company. We weren't trying to cheat anyone. We would even give people brochures that spelled out the exact quality of our wares.

But to avoid jail time, the salesmen had turned state's evidence and tried to pin the scheme on us. Joe, Jeff, and I were charged with five felonies and twenty-three misdemeanors.

Joe and I had to hire a lawyer. We hired a second lawyer for Jeff because, as the direct manager of these two salesmen, he was at the highest level of risk. Joe and I paid for Jeff's attorney on the recommendation of our lawyer.

I was completely panicked and scared.

We didn't have the money to pay for the attorneys. Our business had been successful, but it had only been running for a few months before this. I had to go into debt, including borrowing $10,000 from my parents, to pay the fees. Joe made plans to flee the country if we lost, and I considered going with him.

I couldn't believe this was all happening to me at twenty years old.

After some witty finagling by our attorney to get us the judge that offered the best chance for a positive outcome—getting our first, far less sympathetic judge to recuse himself because he had a conflict of interest—the trial began. I was worried and anxious, but very quickly, it became clear the district attorney had nothing. Even the judge said our business sounded like a good one.

In the end, we were found not guilty of all the charges, except Jeff, who was charged with one misdemeanor and went on probation for six months. That was all so the district attorney had something to save face, and we could be sure the case was behind us.

We had gotten out of it. Of course, I was happy and relieved. But the cost of this experience would linger for many more years. In fact, the fallout of it all is what led to my first real crisis.

CHAPTER 4

DARK NIGHT OF THE SOUL

I WASN'T GOING TO JAIL, BUT THAT DIDN'T MEAN THINGS were going well.

I tried to resurrect The Chain Gang after the police confiscated everything. I bought more product and refurnished the office. But at the time, our business was infamous. No one wanted to work for us, and no one wanted to buy from us. I started selling everything in the office just to survive.

My relationship with Sandy also dissolved. She told me that once the court case was over, she wanted me to move out.

"I thought this was working," I said.

"Mark, just because it works for you doesn't mean it works for me," she said.

Beyond the heartache, a breakup with Sandy was a housing crisis. I didn't have the money to find another place.

I had borrowed a lot of money to cover everyone's court fees. Now, I didn't have any source of income to pay it back or to live on. I borrowed more from my parents and Jeff's mom. In desperation, I went to Jeff's divorced father, who was worth millions, but he had no interest in helping financially, even though I'd helped keep his son out of prison.

"Mark, anything short of money I can do for you, let me know," he had said. His son and I were facing life in prison, and all he wanted to offer was support. It still bothers me thinking about that conversation.

Joe moved out of town to find a job. Jeff went back to Los Angeles to be close to his parents. Sandy also got a new job. Jamie wasn't talking to me because I hadn't told him about my second business.

That left me broke, lonely, and isolated. At times I spiraled to a point when I didn't think I'd get out again. The sadness and pain became unbearable. I had no friends, no girlfriend, no business, and no money. All I had was debt. Lots of it.

There was something else missing in my life at this time as well—any spirituality to speak of. That connection that had preoccupied my mind and been with me during some of the hardest times of my childhood was simply absent in my life at this point. I was too broken to accept any of those forces. So I just abandoned them. Without even realizing it, this contributed to the emptiness that gnawed at my soul. It would take me years to recover.

SIX MONTHS OF TEARS

After moving out of Sandy's, I rented a cheap apartment on my own and began to wander around Santa Clara, crying all the time. The tears just wouldn't stop.

I felt so alone. I was so desperate for human connection that I went to get a library card just to have a conversation with the librarian. I longed for someone to talk to.

This went on for months.

After crying more tears than I thought humanly possible, I finally ended up at a mental health clinic in San Jose. The therapist came out and greeted me.

"What can I do for you?" she asked.

"I'm depressed. My life is falling apart. I need help," I said, crying again.

"Are you suicidal?" she asked.

"I think about it, but I'm not going to do it," I admitted to her.

She looked at me over the brim of her glasses. "Well, you can't stay here," she said bluntly and unsympathetically. Then, she simply looked down at her clipboard and went back to her office.

I just sat there, with nowhere else to go. All I could do was keep crying.

THE BREAKDOWN

My parents finally loaned me some money in an attempt to help me get back on my feet. I rented an apartment in Santa Clara and brought with me the only piece of furniture I owned—a big walnut desk from the old Chain Gang office. The problem was, I had no way to transport this massive object, and so I hitchhiked with it across the city. You can imagine how ridiculous that looked.

Eventually, a pickup driver stopped—probably half out of sympathy and half out of curiosity—and gave me a ride. He even helped me carry the desk up the stairs to my apartment.

In my new apartment, I slept on the floor. I'd taken up that practice after I had first moved out of my parents' house. I found sleeping on the floor kept my back straighter. That was one of my few lucky breaks, seeing as I couldn't afford a mattress anyway.

I may have had a roof over my head, but the crying continued. In total, it lasted for six months straight. My coping mechanism was washing counters. I probably had the cleanest kitchen and bathroom you've ever seen. Any time I felt tears coming on, I would get out a rag and start scrubbing. Handling the water, it seemed, really helped. I still had that same connection to water in my moments of sadness that I'd had as a child. The only difference was I no longer fit into the sink.

I tried to move on and find a job—and at that time, I would take anything, really. I applied to record stores and bookshops, but no one called me back. So I continued walking. And crying. And scrubbing. Sometimes, I'd call Mom and share my pain with her for thirty minutes at a time. She told me she was willing to do anything for me—except let me move back home.

Then, one day, I was visiting Sandy's and my heart began to hurt. This wasn't a new thing—it had happened before. Each previous time, Sandy would say, "You need to see someone about that," and I'd say, "I know, I will." But then the pain would stop. This time, though, was different. The pain didn't go away, and it was getting worse. I knew something was really wrong.

I called my mother and told her I needed to do something. My body was breaking down. I wanted to come home, but she refused.

"You can't come home," she said, "but I'll pay for therapy."

You see, my parents could get along if us kids weren't around. My father was so competitive, he'd upset the whole family if any of the sons were home. That cut me off from the house. But I would take any help I could get.

I started seeing my first therapist, Dr. Gail Frankel, a Freudian psychologist in San Jose, but our sessions were pointless. They didn't help me at all except to provide a distraction when I flirted with her. I needed to make a change—I needed someone who could really challenge me. That was my only hope for any kind of recovery.

DR. BRAVIN'S WISDOM

I told Paul about my trouble with Dr. Frankel, and he suggested I consider Dr. Martin Bravin. He had been my mother's therapist first. He was the one to convince my mom to stop hitting us. Once she stopped going, she sent Paul to see him. Paul had become such a problem child, skipping school and forging notes from my parents, that Mom had delivered an ultimatum: get therapy or get out of the house.

Paul liked Dr. Bravin, though, and he thought I would, too. "The guy just talks a lot," Paul explained. "We talk about everything, even science."

I decided that might be just what I needed. But I needed something else, too, and that was to move home. Living alone in my apartment just wasn't working, and Dr. Bravin was too far away to commute. Despite her reservations, I convinced my mom to let me move home, with the understanding that it was temporary. She gave me a thousand dollars to buy a junky old Mercedes to drive myself home and agreed to pay for Dr. Bravin while I slept on her and Dad's living room floor. After therapy, I was to get a job and be back on my way.

Dr. Bravin was probably in his fifties when I started seeing him. He was a gestalt therapist, with a calm, no-nonsense demeanor. For all that, he had an inviting attitude, with his pleasant heaviness and salt and pepper hair and beard. I remember enjoying the deep, thoughtful tone of his voice. He could have been a rabbi.

Almost immediately, I could feel the healing begin.

During my first session, I told Dr. Bravin my story. He listened attentively, and when I was through, he paused before saying, "Here's what I think."

He took out a puzzle and put it on the coffee table between us. It was a puzzle of his face cut out in big pieces. He took the pieces apart and threw them in all different directions.

"This is you," he said. "Your problem is that you won't go back together the same way. That's what we're going to do here. We're going to find a new way to put you together."

It sounded simple, but it was extremely meaningful to me. For so long, I had tried to put myself and my life back together the way they were before, only to find it didn't work. I now knew that was because it was impossible.

For the first time in a long while, Dr. Bravin pushed me to confront material life through a spiritual lens. It was the nudge I needed to move past my struggles and get on with my life—and slowly start to let the spiritual back in.

"What do you want?" Dr. Bravin asked.

"To be centered," I answered. By that, I meant I didn't want to cry all the time. I wanted to feel in control again. Perhaps I meant even more. Dr. Bravin grasped it all.

"If you want that feeling all the time, you have a couple options," Dr. Bravin said. "You can take martial arts and maybe achieve it in ten years. Or, you can take two weekends and do Erhard Seminar Training (est)." The est training is a course that teaches principles to inspire transformation in your life.

In the meantime, he gave me some powerful ideas to work with.

First was to banish the shoulds, can'ts, and won'ts in my everyday speech. "Watch your language," he coached. "Don't tell me you *can't* do something. Tell me you're unwilling or unable to at the moment. Because you are *able* to."

These ideas just clicked. In fact, I changed my language right away. It reoriented how I thought. I realized the only person I could change was me. The only circumstance I could control was my own. No one else could have power over my life and thoughts.

Dr. Bravin encouraged me to put my pieces back together in a new way through being present, telling the truth, facing my fears, and above all, through writing. He taught me to see things as they are and not how I would have them be. Aside from being distraught and depressed, my mind remained extremely fragmented. He asked me to write for an hour a day, but I couldn't do it. There were too many voices, I couldn't focus.

He pushed for thirty minutes, but I still struggled. My mind was firing all at once, and I couldn't turn it off. Finally, he said try for just five minutes.

That, I found, I could do, although at first I wrote in massive letters with only thirty words on the page. But slowly, my mind cleared. In time, my writing got smaller and neater, and I could write for longer periods—I went from getting one page to two and then three.

The writing helped. I started to become someone I wanted to recognize again. My pieces were coming back together. And perhaps it also unlocked something else, a conduit to powerful voices trying to contact me—but that type of writing was still ahead.

Dr. Bravin also helped me confront my past and my relationship with my parents. Though they had never provided me with intimacy, I had never confronted them about it. I couldn't face the idea of saying how I felt to them, particularly my father. Dr. Bravin had me do a gestalt exercise to make this possible. Whenever my dad came up and I had something to say to him, Dr. Bravin would pull up a chair and tell me to imagine my father in it. My dad wasn't actually there, but in my psyche, he was. So it felt real, and I became very activated.

With my dad in that chair, I began to accuse him of all the things he had done that damaged me. "You never said you loved me," I'd say, and immediately start to cry. I'd then switch chairs, playing out the scene as my father. It was unbelievably hard and extremely painful, but it worked. I found myself beginning to let go of the deep hurt I held onto from my childhood. I was learning to show up in life where I had shut down in the past.

After a number of months, I convinced myself I was healed. I decided to leave therapy.

"I think I'm done," I told Dr. Bravin at my last appointment.

He just looked at me and said, "You haven't even started."

He was absolutely right, but I was afraid to go where he wanted me to go. I had put enough of myself back together that I felt I could fake it again. It would be a long journey ahead before I was truly whole.

HALF-STEPS BACK INTO THE WORLD

I may have stopped seeing Dr. Bravin regularly, but I didn't forget what he taught me. After I left his office, I called the est training and registered for the next seminar. I asked my mom to cover the fee.

I made other efforts to build on my growth after therapy, as well. I took a course on Silva Mind Control, where I learned to program my psyche and document my dreams. I also attended some gestalt marathon group therapy sessions—these were eighteen-hour-long events that wore you down through tiredness until you spoke your true thoughts.

Most of the people in the therapy sessions were two or three times my age, and they would often admire me for joining at such a young age. "You're doing this at twenty?" they'd say. "Yeah, I'm fucked up at twenty," was my response.

Some of these groups had real value, others less so, but I wasn't in a position to take in those values at the time. More than anything, what I got from those groups was how much more work I had ahead.

In fact, for all my intention to be "done" with this period of my life, I continually saw how little progress I'd made and how much more work there was ahead. I was still living with my parents, and I still didn't have a job. Only now, when I was probably in good enough shape to take a basic job, I was no longer as willing to settle for just any gig. I wanted to create my own work. I knew my future included running my own business. And I wanted to jump right back into that world.

My first thought was to open a niche clothing shop. I became enamored with Victorian clothing and was lucky enough to come upon some vacant storefronts about a mile from my parents' house. The stores had been decorated with an old western look, and I decided one would be perfect for my next venture—I would open a Victorian clothing store. I borrowed $10,000 from my parents to lease one of the stores and go on a shopping spree for my inventory. Then…I never opened the store.

I just couldn't do it. I couldn't face the possibility of going months without a customer—a common occurrence for new businesses, particularly in Los Angeles. "Who wants to buy Victorian clothing other than me?" I asked myself. I psyched myself out of the whole thing before I'd even tried—though not, unfortunately, before I spent all the money on inventory.

At the root of it, I was still scared. I'd been so scarred by the court case, I was terrified of failure, or worse. I couldn't take the potential debt. But if I was to stay living with my parents, I had to do *something*. That was my mom's new condition for me as she became resigned to my continued presence. And without a job or a business, that meant one thing—I had to study.

I enrolled at the same junior college Martin had gone to and went on to take more classes at another college nearby the year after. I studied psychology, humanities, and business, and I enjoyed it. I got all A's, but I soon became terribly bored. My main interest was learning enough to start my next business (whatever it would be) on a better footing. But the material wasn't designed for someone like me. I already knew most of what they were teaching because I had run my own company before. I decided if I was going to be a businessman, I had to get back into business.

But I still couldn't get anything going. I moved from one place to another, living with my parents, my brother, and even for a time with Sandy, although only as friends now. Ideas came and went, but there was little progress.

Until I reconnected with Jerry.

Jerry was living in New York City and was still bitter about his cousin, Jamie, choosing me as a business partner for The Chain Reaction over him. But he was willing to mend burnt bridges and invited me to come visit during the Christmas holiday and check out a cookie business he was starting up.

When I got out there, I saw that Jerry had the bones of a business, but he was shy about starting it. He had the money (from his dad) and a warehouse full of cookie carts, but he had no cookies and no one to work for him. He said he was waiting to start after winter.

We came up with a solution. We could simply buy cookies in a store, warm them up in the cookie cart oven, and sell them on the street. People would pay the extra charge for a warm cookie, even if it wasn't our recipe. I was confident it would work.

"Well, let's get out there," I urged Jerry. So we bought some cookies, and I mustered the courage to sell them on the streets of Manhattan.

It was a success. We sold a bunch of cookies. I had finally dipped my toe back into the business world, and it felt really good.

After I dropped out of college, I moved to New York to help Jerry manage his business. We lived together in a small loft above the warehouse with only a nine-inch TV and a tiny shower. I slept in the stairwell, and Jerry slept in the loft. It was one of the best times of my life. I felt free. I had few pressing or intense responsibilities. I oversaw the daily management of the business, but I was relieved that it wasn't my company. I just read and thought and talked to people on the streets. And sold cookies, brought our sales people fresh cookies, and gave them bathroom breaks.

I even got my own cookie cart. It was my first concrete step back into business—and into life.

THE FIRST AWAKENING

Aside from running the business in New York City, I kept life pretty simple. I didn't drink or smoke, so I didn't have much to do. In the evenings, Jerry and I would often go out to the movies and the theater.

One night, we went to see *Heart Beat*, a movie about Jack Kerouac. When we came out of the theater, I just started crying. It wasn't the movie that brought this on. It was something deeper and more expansive. Nor were these the hot tears I had from those months of depression. They weren't tears of desperation, depression, or loss. They were the cold tears of *joy*.

Jerry and his girlfriend, Carol, looked at me, concerned and asked what was wrong.

"You don't get it?" I cried. "Everything is perfect. Everything is going to work out. Everything is about love."

They both looked at me like I was crazy. I couldn't explain it, but a shift had occurred in me. For the first time, I was experiencing an Awakening. In that moment, I reconnected with the spiritual world, and in reconnecting, I felt greater clarity about life and existence than I ever had before. This went beyond glimpses of the future or awareness of past lives. I felt plugged into the whole conception of the universe, across every dimension. I soon realized that there is nothing to be known that is not already contained within us.

It was the end of my spiritual isolation, and the spark of a renewed connection to God and the greater reality at work in my life and in every life.

WHAT IS AWAKENING?

The moment I experienced after the movie in New York was one of Awakening, but it wasn't a *Complete* Awakening. Complete Awakening comes not in a flash of insight or an "ah-ha" moment that soon dissipates. Instead, it occurs when you no longer strive for further knowledge because all realization has been integrated—you actually realize and associate with the Supreme Cause of All Causes. Of course, this is a lofty goal, one that even Buddha and Jesus took a lifetime (if not many lifetimes) to achieve.

In the words of Sri Bhaktivedanta Swami:

"The difference between Self-Realization and material illusion is to know that the temporary or illusory impositions of material energy in the shape of gross and subtle bodies are superficial coverings of the self. The coverings take place due to ignorance. Such coverings are never effective in the person of the Personality of Godhead. Knowing this convincingly is called liberation, or seeing the Absolute."

At the center of this realization—as I correctly felt in my short-lived first awakening—is love. To describe that experience I rely upon a verse from the Bible, specifically 1 John 4:18:

"There is no fear in love. But perfect love drives out fear, because fear has to do with punishment. The one who fears is not made perfect in love."

Or, as the psychologist Helen Schucmann puts it in her book, *A Course in Miracles*:

Perfect love casts out fear.
If fear exists,
Then there is not perfect love.

But

Only perfect love exists.
If there is fear,
It produces a state that does not exist.

My first experience with perfect love would not meet the strict definitions of complete Awakening, but it was a sign I was returning to the path that could lead to it. This was only a taste of what was to come.

Along the way, I would have more trials. Most people suffer three dark nights in their lives. I have had two so far, the second of which we will encounter in time. I am certain that these nights are the subtle foundations of one's waking up—the darkness that blends with the light of love.

THE BATTLE BETWEEN LIGHT AND DARK

If I hadn't had the conflict that I did with Staz in Toronto, I doubt that I ever would have believed in "dark" forces or entities like those talked about in ancient scriptures. People used to ask me why I didn't change the name of my horse, Lucifer. I'd reply because it means "to carry light." That is the primary association I have with the name, aside from its connection to my noble friend.

That is not to say that there isn't evil in the world. There is, and it comes from us—and, indeed, the Divine. For anything to be possible, it must originate within the Absolute. This is the duality in which we live. Within all of us is both darkness and light. The makings of good and evil. We have the free will to choose what we want to cultivate. The more we associate with goodness and light, the more we will cultivate that light. And to the contrary, if we are attracted to evil and negative energy, that is what we will attract and how we will see the world. It is all happening within the mind.

In my early adult years, after facing so many trials and tribulations that seemed to come out of nowhere, I had to accept that this darkness must have been something that I previously attracted. If it wasn't, then I did not have any free will. That would make me a victim of circumstances for the rest of my life. So, I decided that I had to work to become a better human being, regardless of the situations that I found myself in. I had to take responsibility for whatever arose. Like people in prison quickly learn, if you want to be happy, the only real freedom that one has, is how you react to all that life has to bring.

We first have to accept "what is," so that we can become present. Then, we can decide if and how we would like to be in any particular situation. We can only change our own response. But we can't change another person. It is up to them to decide.

Why would we pursue and attract dark thoughts? After all, shouldn't we all want to live and think in the light? It is not that simple. Until your consciousness is free from the shadows of birth and death, you will continue into the unknown at death. This creates a fearful state for one who is embodied. This fear welcomes dark thoughts to emerge within one's consciousness. This is why we must take this opportunity to realize our own Divine nature and to let go of the darkness. This will allow us to see our own true nature.

The terror and anger we feel are our own efforts to evade being completely awake. We wander ambiguously in the landscape of our own mind. If we recognize these projections, liberation is instantaneous.

We all must work through the darkness that is lying deep within our psyches. This is usually done through dreams and conscious awareness of one's states of being.

Jesus instructs us to resist not evil. He suggests this due to the fact that we are already living in a world of uncertainty. If we resist evil, we are in essence sharing our own dark energy and reawakening any evil that is lying dormant within our consciousness. If not dealt with properly, this fear may drag us into more uncertainty than we are already feeling.

It is always best to associate with the positive light of the world.

Or to get guidance from one who has overcome these states. This is what Jesus was doing in the "wilderness" of his mind. When Satan—or the "adversary," or that which opposes, which is the meaning of that word in Hebrew and Aramaic)—the mind tried to tempt Jesus back into mundane consciousness, Jesus wasn't interested. Jesus had finally overcome the world by remembering only God on the cross, overcoming the greatest fear, death.

CHAPTER 5

A SON OF LIGHT

IN SOME WAYS, THE STORY I'M ABOUT TO TELL YOU IS ONE of the most boring ones you can imagine: I met a girl. We had a connection. We went out a few times. It didn't work out. The end.

I'm sure many people reading this could tell a similar tale. But, like most of the events in my life, there's more to it than what you see on the surface.

At this time in my life, I had returned from New York with a renewed sense of spirituality, so much so that I began doing psychic readings and past life regressions for people in the Los Angeles area. I embraced my revived connection with the spiritual world—it was a breath of fresh air after the trouble I had endured the years prior. But what I didn't expect with this homecoming was the cosmic battle that was beginning to brew, a clash of light and dark I never saw coming.

After I had been back in California a few days, I decided to spend some time in Toronto and stay with Martin while he studied at the university there.

Before leaving on this trip, my mother and I went to the

Bodhi Tree bookstore so I could get some reading material. At that time, the Bodhi Tree was the only "New Age" alternative bookstore in Los Angeles. Since my funds were limited, I always checked out the "used" section first. Sandy had told me about a book that I might like, but I couldn't remember the title. I paced the rows of shelves, but just couldn't find it. Giving up, I chose another title.

At the cash register my mother asked, "Did you find what you were looking for?"

As I turned to reply, a book caught the corner of my eye. It was sticking out from the other books halfway off the shelf: *The Aquarian Gospel of Jesus the Christ*.

That was the book that I was looking for!

With the book in hand, I felt ready for the trip. But on the day of my departure, I felt an incredibly uneasy, scared feeling inside me. I meditated and was assured that I was going to be ok. But after I arrived at the airport, I couldn't bring myself to board the plane. I found a payphone and called Sandy, who was still my close friend, to tell her how scared I felt.

"I know the feeling isn't because the plane is going to crash, so I'm going anyway," I told her. "But *something* is going to happen."

"Why not take another flight?" she suggested.

"This is the only flight. I have to go."

Suddenly, she caught that same fear that I was experiencing. She said, "Mark, I know you don't believe, but I want you to tell me that you accept Christ as your Savior."

To my surprise, despite being brought up Jewish, this wasn't difficult. As I said it, my body instantaneously became filled with a burst of light from within. I could physically see the light and was overwhelmed with peace. Knowing that I was going to be ok, I thanked Sandy and boarded the plane.

But I was still somewhat dazed and couldn't shake the feeling that something I wasn't prepared for was still going to happen.

MEETING THE DEVIL AT THE BORDER

I spent the first few days in Toronto wandering around the city during the day and sleeping on Martin's living room floor at night. He had roommates who would come and go at all hours of the night, and it didn't take me long to grow tired of that arrangement.

I decided to visit some friends who lived in Upstate New York and take a bus so I could visit Niagara Falls along the way. I took The Aquarian Gospel of Jesus the Christ with me. It had become my close companion on this trip. It was fascinating to me—not only did it teach me about Jesus in the Gospels, but it also covered Jesus in India. Excited to finish it on the bus route to New York—but timorous about reading about the crucifixion—I settled into my seat.

As I sat down, though, I caught a glimpse of a girl a few rows away. I felt an instant connection to her, an attraction unlike anything I'd experienced before. I knew I *had* to get next to her.

All passengers deboarded the bus to pass through customs, and when we reboarded, I sat down next to the girl. Completely infatuated, we talked the rest of the trip. I learned her name was Anastasia—and went by Staz—and she lived in Toronto.

"If you're coming back, you should visit," she said. I felt my heart jump at the idea of getting together with her again.

As Anastasia and I got off the bus at our destination and gathered our luggage, we continued to talk. I still couldn't take my eyes off of her as we walked through the bus station until suddenly, I panicked—I'd left my book on the bus!

"What's the big deal?" she said, looking at me like I was crazy. "It's just a book."

She didn't understand what the book meant to me—or perhaps she understood all too well and delighted in parting me from the wisdom within it.

I was distraught. Still, we exchanged numbers. We met once while I was in New York, but Staz, previously so interested and flirtatious, was suddenly distant and standoffish. It was an uncomfortable experience.

Returning to Toronto, I felt sick. Yet I still felt compelled to call her again.

When we went out, I told her I did psychic readings and past life regressions in Los Angeles. She interrupted me before I could say any more.

"Reveal something to me about myself," she said.

I looked at her and, suddenly, I felt extremely afraid. This had never happened to me before while doing a reading.

Closing my eyes and taking a few deep breaths, I felt calm and centered. Opening my eyes again, I saw Staz was gazing into mine. I looked back into her eyes, and my fear turned to terror. I couldn't speak. The voice of reason within told me to get out! I was feeling as if I was going to be stabbed in the heart, a pair of scissors on the screen of my mind. More than once I glanced down at her hands even though I knew that they were empty.

"What do you see?" she asked. I couldn't even look at her. I didn't know what to say. I just kept looking at her hands, thinking there was a chance she'd pull a knife and stab me, that's how afraid I was.

"Do you want me to tell you about you?" she asked, seeing I was clearly struggling.

"Sure," I replied.

"You're of the light, and I'm of the dark," she said. "We're going to do battle in the not-too-distant future."

I laughed, trying to make light of it. "Yeah, right, okay," I said.

"You don't know who you are, do you?" she went on. "Or who I am. I work with Satan."

I admitted I didn't know who I was. What I did know, though, was that my heart was shaking inside my chest.

"Who will win?" I asked.

"You will."

"What will happen to you?"

She shrugged. "I'll be dead."

"Then why do you talk with me?"

"I love the cat and mouse!" I have to admit, that when I heard these words I knew as uncomfortable as it was, that there was something true in it for me as well. Apparently we were biding our time until we were ready.

And Staz was fine biding it as comfortably as possible.

"You can stay at my place, but you don't have to," she said. The way she dangled the offer out there only added to my discomfort, but just as dark forces have always attracted spirits, I still felt drawn to her sexually. So we went to her house to have tea.

When we arrived, the house was dark except for just a few candles burning.

"Don't you turn on any lights?" I asked. No, she said, just looking at me in all seriousness. She invited me to sleep in her bed, and as I lay next to her, I felt nothing but coldness. There was no love; no loving energy emanated from her body. I realized she must be holding on to a lot of pain to be like this. When I tried to instigate some type of touch—to act on the attraction that clearly existed between us—she showed no reception. She just wanted to sleep. So I slept on her floor.

The next morning, I opened a drape to let some light in. Staz grabbed the drape from my hand. "If you want light, go outside," she said coldly. She closed the drape, but not before I caught a glimpse of the graveyard outside of her house.

As I walked back to Martin's, I could feel the hurt in my body from this encounter. By the time I arrived back at his place, a deep pain had settled in my chest, like I had a knife in my heart. I couldn't look down at it because when I did, it felt like the knife would twist.

I started crying and had a vision of myself dressed in a skirt like the men of ancient Egypt wore. I was being flogged. These pains continued throughout the day and I had trouble distracting my mind from it. As the time neared for Staz and I to meet, I felt even worse. We had agreed to meet outside of a subway stop close to the restaurant where we were going for dinner. As the time to go neared, the stabbing pressure in my heart increased.

"God, are you there?" I asked.

With my eyes closed, I saw a blue light with a white star. God. I could feel Him with me. But when I opened my eyes again, I immediately felt the pain in my heart.

Despite the pain, Staz and I agreed to meet up again. The inexplicable attraction kept pulling me in. We met for dinner, and she asked me to look in her eyes and read who she was again.

All I saw was evil.

But I also noticed the first signs of defeat. Her words to me confirmed the matter.

"I can't take it anymore!" she said. "You're my total opposite. You radiate love and light, and I can't stand it!"

The encounters with Anastasia broke off. She told me that if we kept meeting, it would end badly for her. I didn't believe her. The pain was such in my heart, I was certain I was the one who was going to die.

To try and get myself through, I started writing about these events. When I wrote, I found myself titling them "Advents as I've Experienced Them," instead of "events." "Advent" means the second coming of Christ. It was an odd word for me to use—fascination with Christ or not.

As I looked more closely, though, the writings were littered with these slips, words like purgatory that had Divine associations but that meant nothing to me...yet.

AUTOMATIC WRITINGS

After my experience with Staz, I didn't know if I would make it back to Los Angeles—I really thought I might die. But I did make it back, and my encounter with that satanic force led to an unexpected development in my spiritual encounters.

One night, I was sitting in my parents' living room, when something suddenly felt very, very wrong. I fell to the floor and cried out to Jesus, begging him for help.

Immediately, my crying stopped. The negative feeling just washed away. A voice within told me to pick up paper and pen and to write.

It was a message to my friend, Sandy:

"A message to Sandra of the Sauers: Hark, I hear you crying and you never go unheard for you are loved and answered in time of need. For wants are of human standing and need no assistance.

"I come to you only to assist and guide you of your will and destination. Don't leave before your time and don't lose faith. For I am by your side at all times.

"I worship the same as you, and He hears your cries. For you do not pray all one (alone)."

It continued like this for two pages and was signed Simon Peter.

I wrote the entire writing in a minute. The vernacular didn't reflect how I write, think, or speak. In fact, as I read it, it made no sense to me. I didn't recognize it as coming from me at all. And how could I? It was signed in another person's name.

I called Sandy and asked if I could read it to her. "It says it's to you," I told her.

Upon hearing it, Sandy identified it as an automatic writing. She said she had really needed to hear that message and asked me to send it to her.

After that first experience, these writings kept happening. I'd be sleeping and I'd hear a voice telling me to get a piece of paper and write something down. The more I did it, the more I realized someone was talking to me from another dimension. Different voices communicated to me and shared various messages, often using words from different religions I didn't even recognize.

This connection to the Divine came through in my dreams, as well. Around this time, I started reading the Bible. I found I could only get through a chapter before falling asleep, and then I would dream of what I read. These weren't acts of the imagination. I was there. Sometimes, I was a person in the story. Sometimes, I watched the story happen from a distance.

I started reading my writings to others to see their reaction. Everyone who heard one was moved. Often, they'd start shaking. It was like the energy attached to where these writings came from woke something up in them.

Around this time, I met a musician named Melinda through Jeff.

Melinda recognized that I had an honest psychic ability and soon began bringing her friends over for me to do psychic readings and past life regressions. Later, Melinda told me there were enough people who wanted to follow me that they wanted me to start a church in the area. I had no interest in becoming the leader of some spiritual organization. I knew that wasn't my path. Still, this was another sign that I was once more on the spiritual path I was meant to walk.

I was finally using my spiritual connection—my light—to help others.

SAINT MARK

Just as the past life regressions I performed intensely affected others, I also had experiences during this time that deeply affected me—and convinced me of my close connection with Jesus. It had been striking while in Toronto how I had struggled to read about Christ's crucifixion in *The Aquarian Gospel of Jesus the Christ*. This wasn't squeamishness on my part, it was because my connection to that event was far more direct.

During the first past life regression I allowed someone to do on me, I found myself watching Jesus being crucified. I couldn't believe the intense pain I felt watching him suffer.

Having grown up Jewish, Jesus was the last person I expected to show up in my past life, yet here he was. I felt so close to him—almost like a brother. I had more regressions performed on me by others, and the same vision continued to come up. Numerous psychics told me if I wasn't an author of one of the Gospels, I certainly had a close connection to Jesus. I never revealed my past learnings when I went to these readings, which suggested the connection must be real.

Other experiences confirmed this link, as well.

When I slept, I'd have visions that transported me to other realms. One vision showed me going through customs as I entered a country like Pakistan or Afghanistan. I was carrying a book in one hand and a church in the other. Many years later, I learned that monks carried small churches in their travels. But in my vision, when I looked down, both were gone. I wandered through old markets searching for my church, when I saw someone in a back alley. He was dressed in a tattered white robe, and as I got closer, I could see that his clothing was stained with blood and dirt. His eyes were dark and had black and blue rings around them. He wore a crown of thorns and was bleeding from a number of spots on his head, ribs, wrists, and feet.

I ran up to him in fear, trembling and with tears in my eyes, saying, "Jesus, Christ, Lord, someone stole my book and church, and I want to get them back. They are important to me, and I know you can tell me where they are!"

He looked at me, not even taking notice of my trembling fear, and spoke, "Don't worry yourself. No one took anything from you. Be glad, for all things return from where they have originated."

With a loving gaze, he smiled at me and said, "You're Saint Mark."

It scared me to hear him say that, but in that fear, my alignment with Jesus grew. Jesus then said "Well, have you seen thine scripture?" In frustration, I replied that I had a Bible and ran away.

I returned to the place where I had left my bags. A woman was now lying on a bed in the front room. My book was underneath it. I blurted out loud, "That's my book!" To which she replied that she tried reading it but couldn't understand a word of it. To which I replied, "Those that know, do."

Around the same time, I received an automatic writing addressed to myself. It said that I was a "Son of the light" and that I could receive messages from "on high."

Vintage image of Jesus discovered in India

After I received it, I borrowed Jeff's car to drive down to The Bodhi Tree Bookstore to see if I could learn more. There was a book there, *The Book of Knowledge: The Keys to Enoch*. The cover contained only the Hebrew name of God, YHWH. It was an expensive book, locked up in a cabinet. As I paged through, I saw that this book wasn't an easy read. It was written in English but looked like Hebrew, and it contained channeled information from another galaxy. I went to give the book back when I saw a woman in her seventies looking at me from across the room.

"I'm being told that you should give that book another chance," she said, nodding at the heavy text still in my hands.

"Okay," I said skeptically. "And who are you?"

"I used to work for Jesus, but now I *actually* work for Him," she said. "I was a nun my whole life, but I've left the church because it has nothing to do with what Jesus is all about."

"I'm going to tell you something else, too," she continued. "You're going to have to be really careful about who you have sex with. If you join up with someone in that manner, you carry their energy for a long time."

If it hadn't been clear how close I came with Staz before, it was clear now.

She kissed me on my third eye and left. I bought the book, despite it being well beyond my means at the time.

I opened the book again. On the first page I looked at, it said:

"The keys to the *"sons of light"* are given in the transmissions of "living energy codes" within the "people of God." They are sent from living universe to living universe to reveal the codes of light, to the orders of evolving species within cellular time so that the coded nuclei membranes may attach with the "larger membrane of universes."

Verse two continued:

"You, as "a believer", can receive modulates, gravitational wave factors that are sent from a Higher Evolutionary Master intelligence of light. This transmissions of knowledge contain codes of light that give you the realization of God's purpose and recognition of where we are in relation to the larger evolving universe."

I was in disbelief. The writing had been true, the proof here, in this book. If I needed confirmation my acceptance of Jesus had shielded me from the darkness that raged around me, this was it. I had forgiveness; I had protection. Seemingly, I *was* a Son of light.

MEETING MY GURU

While my connection with Jesus was clear, I would often still find myself in tears, overwhelmed, and afraid by my lack of understanding about everything going on with me.

Jesus, himself, felt too far in the past to help me comprehend. So one night, I cried to Him, asking Him to send me someone more contemporary for guidance.

Once again, Jesus answered my pleas. Instantly, my crying stopped. It suddenly occurred to me to read the book that Pat had shown me all those years ago, *Autobiography of a Yogi*. There, I learned about Yogananda, who was sent by the great guru Mahavatar Babaji to the West to teach yoga in the light of Christianity.

I read *Autobiography of a Yogi* in a few days, and immediately afterward, signed up to learn kriya yoga at Yogananda's Church of All Religions. Luckily, Yogananda had written everything down because he anticipated that many communities wouldn't have gurus. That is what I was looking for, someone who lived more recently, and whose words I could read directly without having to rely on someone else's interpretation of a text that was already heavily edited, such as the New Testament.

Yogananda taught that you needed to meditate before you can practice kriya yoga, so I started meditating, at first with great difficulty. I kept falling asleep after a few minutes. Eventually, though, I could practice it for hours at a time and my meditations became very deep and meaningful.

I would later find out that my connection to Yogananda was not unique in my family. Jules, the uncle who provided most of the love I experienced in my childhood, had also been attracted to him. Before my parents were ready to move to California, my father had asked Jules to come out first. Unbeknownst to my father, he spent time studying meditation at one of Paramahansa Yogananda's ashrams, meditating with Yogananda's close disciples. For many years, I had known that Jules was well-practiced in using the power of his subconscious mind, but I had no idea that we were on the same path.

When I mentioned to my mother that Jules practiced the meditation techniques of Paramahansa Yogananda, she told me that she knew that Jules was "different." She went on to say that he had once gotten stung by a bee on the inside of his mouth. My mother offered him help, and Jules closed his eyes and whispered a few words. After saying these words, Jules felt no pain and didn't mention the event again.

I later learned that my spiritual-minded uncle was saying the name of Mahavatar Babaji, the great-great guru of Paramahansa Yogananda who on the request of Lord Jesus, sent Yogananda to the West. Yogananda had told his disciples that by merely mentioning Babaji's name with reverence, one would receive a blessing.

With this family pedigree, then, it's hardly surprising that I was so instantaneously attracted to Yogananda.

I started reading books by Yogananda's disciples. When I read about the day Yogananda left his body, I started crying uncontrollably. I was so moved; I felt like I was there.

That same night, Yogananda visited me. Even though he wasn't in a physical body, I could feel his presence, much as I could feel my mother's when, as a sick child, she would sit next to my bed while I moved in and out of consciousness. His presence was awe-inspiring, filling me with love. My body was asleep, but my mind was awake, much as one's subtle awareness is heightened in deep meditation. His presence immediately raised the vibrations within my body.

Standing next to me, Yogananda touched my third eye and told me, "I want you to keep your consciousness here as much as possible."

"But I need wisdom," I responded.

As if in response, I suddenly noticed that Yogananda's guru, Sri Yukteswarji Giri, was also there. Yogananda had always called his guru "an incarnation of wisdom." I realized then that I could get knowledge from him, as well.

I got up and turned to where they were standing. I reached out, expecting to touch them, but instead, all I saw was a cloud of vapor as they faded back into the ether, returning to the dimension in which they reside. The Divine energy of their presence filled my room for months.

This was my initiation as a disciple of Yogananda. Someone like that touches your life for a reason. I accepted his energy into me, and he's been a part of me ever since.

CHECKING PREJUDICE

Some of the wisdom I had to learn was to abandon old assumptions of others and a need to correct those who perceived reality less clearly. Two events in particular drove this wisdom home.

The first piece of instruction came to me through a dream. After my dream visit from Lord Jesus, it started to bug me how Western Christians portrayed Jesus as a White, Anglo-Saxon man with blonde hair and blue eyes. Whenever I had conversations with born-again Christians, I would point out that Jesus did not have a pasty complexion. Rather, he had olive skin, dark hair, and dark eyes. I was adamant about this—until one night when Jesus let me know how he felt about it.

In my dream, I was in the American South. I was walking outside of a small country town and could hear music coming from a nearby farm. I made my way in the dark across a field until I reached the farm house with its large barn lit up for a shindig. When I opened the barn doors, I was surprised to see so many people inside. Everyone was eating, dancing, and having fun!

To my immense surprise, I saw Jesus sitting at one of the picnic tables. I offered my obeisances, touching my head to the ground before His feet as a sign of my respect for Him. The people nearby were watching and seemed shocked. They had never seen anyone do this. Looking around the barn, I noticed that most of the people were dressed in country farm attire. The men wore flannel button-up shirts and blue jeans—and so did Jesus. Not only that, but I now noticed that Jesus had blonde hair and piercing blue eyes. I got up and took a seat across the table from him. I gazed into his loving blue eyes. Jesus looked at me with such warmth and said, "What concern is it to you how they see me?"

I realized then that he was right. It shouldn't matter to me how anyone thought of Him.

A few weeks later, I received another instruction in the form of another dream. This time I was walking down a road where lots of "hillbillies" lived. I was lost and was looking for directions. I came upon a large old convertible. Seated inside were two rather large women. Their hair was disheveled, and they were dressed in old ratty dresses. One of them had her feet up on the dash, and the other had one of her legs hanging over the door. The car was littered with trash. As I asked them for directions, I noticed a book on their dashboard. I could see the title through the windshield. It was titled *The Teachings of Lord Chaitanya*, who was the founder of the original Hare Krishna movement. It looked ragged and well read.

In shock, I blurted out, "You know Lord Chaitanya!"

"Oh yes," they said, "we read that book all the time." And here I had been judging the book by its cover.

A SECOND AWAKENING

Shortly afterward, while practicing physical yoga, I began to see my life more clearly. On a physical level, I felt this kundalini energy—snake energy—shoot through my body. I don't know how I managed it. It normally takes many years of practice, but I felt it shoot through my body, spine, and to the top of my head.

Kundalini energy allowed me to experience complete knowing. I couldn't necessarily explain a complex scientific phenomenon, such as a black hole, but I could understand its deeper implication. I could see the black hole through the lens of the third eye. I could see that all these external discoveries referred to internal truths—most of us just don't recognize them.

Kriya yoga enhanced this understanding, allowing me to feel complete oneness with the universe and provided emotional healing of the traumas I had endured. It ironed out the wrinkles in my psyche that Dr. Bravin hadn't quite straightened out.

I became completely aware of the perfection of each type of creature in the universe. A horse is a perfect example of a horse. A chicken is a master within its own world. Every animal is a genius in their unique realm.

It's the same with humans. Sri Yukteswarji Giri once told me, "You first have to learn to be human," meaning before I embarked on any spiritual work or growth, I needed to understand who I was—spirit-soul. Because, just as a horse or a chicken, we are the perfect example of a human. We have everything we need, it just comes down to if we decide to become aware of it or not.

This was my second awakening. And, unlike the first, which was a fleeting period of recognizing the beauty and love of the universe, this awareness has remained with me.

TWO SPIRITUAL MASTERS

Each person has the potential to have two gurus: the one who initiates you and the one who educates you. It can be the same person, but it doesn't have to be. If someone introduces you to Jesus, for example, they are not necessarily the person who teaches you about Jesus.

Guru means "one who takes you out of darkness and into the light." In other words, it's someone who wakes you up. When Yogananda met his own guru, he asked, "Are you going to show me God?"

The question may seem overly ambitious, but the answer is important because taking a guru is a lifetime commitment—in fact, it's beyond a lifetime. The agreement with a guru is that s/he will follow you through lifetimes if you don't achieve your goals in this lifetime. Yogananda didn't want to commit to his guru until he could be sure he'd show him God.

We see this again in Jesus and John the Baptist. John had been Jesus's guru in previous lives. When they met in the life told in the Gospels, Jesus had surpassed his guru. This is why John felt unworthy to baptize him.

Jesus made this clear when, in Matthew 17:10-11, his disciples asked, "Why then do the teachers of the law say that Elijah must come first?"

Jesus replied, "To be sure, Elijah comes and will restore all things."

As Yogananda made clear in his autobiography, Elijah was the previous incarnation of his guru, John the Baptist, who taught Jesus in his life as Elisha, as we learn in the 1 Kings and 2 Kings in the Old Testament. It was only through that guidance that Jesus could come to surpass his master, "now perfected in Divine realization."

While Yogananda—who taught yoga in the light of Christianity and initiated thousands of practitioners into the practice of Kriya yoga—initiated me into the process of waking up, it was Bhaktivedanta Swami—the founder of the modern Hare Krishna movement, whom I would encounter later—who has provided me with most of my spiritual guidance. He is my instructing spiritual master, whereas Yogananda is my initiating spiritual master.

If you are seeking a guru, you do not have to follow any formal process. You can simply check out different teachers and observe them over time. You can also read spiritual classics and use prayer. Choose whomever attracts your heart. If one is truly sincere, personalities like Jesus will not turn anyone away.

However, once you choose a guru, the goal is to practice the Master's teachings as closely as possible. It doesn't work to commit sins and then chant or repent to nullify the sins, only to go on to repeat them. You must commit to the guru's path.

If you hire a guide to take you to the top of Everest, you don't head off on your own looking for another path. That could be self-destructive. Once you choose the guide, you follow the path they lay out.

CHAPTER 6

MEETING LILA

WITH MY SPIRITUAL CONNECTION BACK IN FULL FORCE, I spent much of my time after my trip to Toronto receiving writings, meditating, and jumping out of my body while reading the Bible.

But the realities of material life were still there. On a very basic level, I needed a place to live.

I had been staying at my parents house in Los Angeles, but I needed a place of my own in the city. So I put an ad in a local classifieds newspaper. "Spiritually minded person, non-smoker, vegetarian looking for a place near the beach," it read.

I was encouraged when I quickly got a call about a place on Venice Beach, but a week before I was to move in, I was told it was no longer available. I was so disappointed. But, just as most things in my life, there was a deeper meaning to that place falling through; a larger plan at play that I didn't know about yet.

The next person I heard from was a woman.

"I'm calling about your ad," she said. "I have a place available for rent in Laguna Beach."

That was further away from Los Angeles than I wanted, I told her. She understood and was about to hang up.

"Wait!" I said, all of a sudden. "Please, don't hang up."

My reaction surprised even me. I wasn't usually so forward with women. But something was telling me to not let this woman hang up that phone.

"Let me check the place out," I said. I had always wanted to live in Laguna Beach—I'd been fond of it ever since I visited the mother of my childhood friend Todd, who had introduced me to juicing. I used to hang out at Todd's mother's house. I loved the area. I just always assumed I couldn't afford it.

"What's your name?" I asked her.

"Lila," she answered, which she pronounced "Leela."

"That's not your real name," I told her.

"How do you know?" she replied, a bit caught off guard by my claim.

"That's what I do," I told her, shrugging on the other end of the line.

"My guru, Bhaktivedanta Swami, gave me that name," she admitted.

Bhaktivedanta Swami, sometimes called Prabhupada, is considered the founder of the modern Hare Krishna movement. He was a messenger of Lord Chaitanya Mahaprabhu, who originated the Hare Krishna practices 500 years ago in India. Interestingly, I had just been reading the *Back to Godhead* magazine, a monthly Hare Krishna publication, that I planned to throw out.

"You can't do that!" she said urgently. "You should keep that." I didn't know at the time the impact Bhaktivedanta Swami Prabhupada would have on my life. He was not yet acting as my instructing guru.

As we talked, I learned Lila was a monk for the Hare Krishnas, but she was planning to move out of the temple. She, her husband, Srinivas, and their five-year-old son, Rama, were living across the street from the temple in an apartment, and she invited me over that weekend to meet her and her family, and to discuss renting a room in the Laguna Beach house.

I knocked on the door that Saturday morning, and Lila answered. She was a strong, fit woman who looked a bit like Jodie Foster. She had a gentle face and wore her hair in a French braid down her back. Behind her, I could see Rama sitting in the kitchen sink playing with water.

"Wow," I thought to myself. "That is *exactly* what I used to do as a child."

It was a sign of the connection I already had with this family, despite having never met any of them before.

I followed Lila in, but soon Srinivas took over the conversation. Srinivas was an artist, and as he showed me his work, which was very impressive, he told me more about my potential future home. It was a house in the hills of Laguna. Primitive but well kept. Lila would be there on weekends to maintain the property, but I'd be the only one living there full time.

Something told me to continue to pursue this place, so I did. The next weekend, I checked it out and decided to take it. I was moving to Laguna Beach.

After a few months, Lila started spending more time in Laguna Beach—and more time with me. This wasn't one-sided interest (either in the house or me). I was also going down to the temple to see her. Despite our clear attraction, though, our relationship remained platonic until she confessed that she and Srinivas were divorcing. After six months of growing close, Lila and I began an affair.

I felt bad at first. I still had a close connection to Jesus, would He approve of this? But Lila reassured me that both she and

Srinivas knew it was over. Srinivas confirmed that later on when he told me he'd ruined the relationship years ago.

Soon, Lila had filed for divorce, and our relationship grew more serious.

BLENDING BELIEFS

I was every bit the "spiritually minded person" I suggested in my ad. And with Lila being a Hare Krishna devotee, we undoubtedly got into some philosophical discussions, even before our affair began.

However, Lila seemed to struggle to hear my ideas out. She saw there was something about me that extended further into the spiritual realm than most. When I read her my automatic writings, she'd start to shake. She shared this same spiritual sensitivity. Yet, her faith had taught her not to trust me and my practices. As a follower of Jesus, Yogananda, and Sri Yukteswarji, I was not particularly orthodox, and the modern Hare Krishna movement didn't recognize the value of any of my spiritual masters.

So I decided to try and understand her using the same source of spiritual knowledge I had always leaned on—reading.

I first dove into Prabhupada's books and found I was drawn to his ideas, even if I wasn't fond of the Hare Krishnas. I (very correctly) felt there was some shady business going on in that organization.

Still, I did not mind using Lila's connection to explore true reality further. Lila worked for the Bhaktivedanta Book Trust, the publishing arm for Iskcon, The International Society of Krishna Consciousness, the Hare Krishnas, and she brought me a translation of the *Bhagavad-gita*. I checked out further translations at the library. I read and compared the different translations of the volumes of work, and found I really liked Prabhupada's translation.

I then started reading the *Śrī Caitanya-caritāmṛta*, comprising nine volumes written by a disciple of Lord Chaitanya Mahaprabhu. It was all biographical and didn't really seem too interesting. But for some reason I couldn't put it down. I would fly through one volume and quickly ask Lila to bring me the next. I was puzzled by my infatuation.

"Why can't I stop reading this?" I asked her. "I don't care about it. I'm not that interested, but I can't stop reading verse after verse."

Lila went to put Rama to bed. Suddenly, I felt my heart fluttering as if I was in love. I felt twitterpated, as they say in the movie *Bambi*.

"Lila, can you come here?" I called.

She came rushing in. "What is it?" she asked.

"Touch me, I need to get grounded," I told her.

She laughed. "These are ecstatic symptoms," she explained, putting her hand on my shoulder. "You just haven't experienced it before. It means you're connecting to Lord Chaitanya."

Lila went to bed. Finally, I couldn't take it anymore. I put the book down, and I just started chanting "Chaitanya Mahaprabhu." All night, through waking and sleeping, I chanted the name. Chaitanya Mahaprabhu, Chaitanya Mahaprabhu, Chaitanya Mahaprabhu.

When Lila and Rama woke up early the next morning, I ran out of the room, "Lila, what can I do? I can't stop chanting this name!"

She told me I had no control over when the chanting would end. "You just have to be with it," she said calmly. "Don't try to make it pass. It will pass in time."

I tried meditating, thinking that might help the feeling leave

my body, but it did just the opposite. The feeling only intensified, to the point that I could feel Lord Chaitanya sitting next
to me, just as I had when Yogananda and Sri Yukteswarji had
come to me. My body was quivering and shaking, I was so
overwhelmed with love.

"I don't know how to reciprocate," I told Lord Chaitanya.
"What can I do for you?"

I could feel his weight as he moved to sit on my lap and laid
his head on my chest, directly over my heart. It felt like a child
nuzzling into their parent's arms as his body melted into mine.

This connection was as powerful as the one I had felt when
accepting Jesus but different in its nature. When I had accepted
Jesus into my heart, it had helped me to overcome my fear and
accept what was meant to be. My loving association with Lord
Chaitanya wasn't based on my need to relive any suffering. His
Mercy transcended all of my previous understanding of love.

It was difficult to explain to others this feeling of pure,
Divine unconditional love I had experienced. They didn't seem
to feel it, even when they tried chanting Lord Chaitanya's name.
I couldn't help but think of how Lord Chaitanya was just like
Jesus, a pure devotee, and I felt I had some association with him
in a previous life, just as I had with Jesus.

I wasn't the only one exploring new beliefs as my and Lila's
relationship grew. Lila, too, tentatively began opening up to the
possibility of expanding her consciousness as our relationship
grew. She had tried to avoid listening to the Yogananda chants
I listened to in the car. But once, when driving on her own, she
chanted along to songs she thought were from her own guru.
She only discovered later that it was the chants of Yogananda.
She realized then that there could be no harm in listening to
Yogananda more often.

Still, she was not yet completely convinced of my direct

spiritual connection to these figures. So I decided to invite her into those experiences.

"Lila, let's dream the future," I told her one day. "God, Lila and I would like to see what is going to happen. Could you show us in a dream?"

We both had these profound dreams about the chaos that was coming—and that is still coming—to our larger society. It involved civil unrest. We saw Highway 5 was closed, and we had to provide documentation that we lived in Oregon to get through. The roads around Los Angeles were so crowded and though everyone wanted to leave, only a few people could get out.

At the time, every part of this vision was confusing. There was no massive unrest in our society. I didn't have any plans to move and had no idea *why* I was dreaming of Oregon. I would soon learn, though, that these visions had meaning—and they'd affect decisions and events in my and Lila's lives for years to come.

KRISHNA IS GOD

Even though Yogananda talked about worshiping Krishna and Lila was part of an organization that proudly sang His name, I had never been willing to see Krishna as God. Growing up Jewish, I was comfortable with a Jewish conception of God. It wasn't a huge leap from there to seeing Jesus as God. I could accept Krishna had a place in the universe, but God? I wasn't so sure.

As our lives and beliefs melded, my religious activities came to encompass Lila's practice as well as my own. I would get up before Lila and Rama and do my meditation and kriyas. Then, when they got up, I'd chant with them. These practices in and of themselves did not draw me closer to Krishna. My thinking was, if Krishna was God, I was going to need Him to show it to me.

One night, I had a dream in which I was walking through a dark jungle. I came across a big monolith of deities. I looked up to see the stone faces of gods that people had worshiped over all of history. I looked down and saw a stream of water coming out of the center of the stone. I saw a light coming out. I bent down to figure out the source of the water, and there I saw Krishna playing his flute. The water was flowing from beneath His feet. I smiled. He saw me, and He smiled.

I woke up and thought, "Krishna is the source of everything."

At the time, I thought the images that took shape in that dream were unique to my own experience. Years later, though, I saw a painting of Krishna in India that shows the same image.

A month went by, and my faith in Krishna began to wane. It was just one dream. Maybe I had just made it up.

But then there was another dream. The Vedas talk about the union of Krishna and Radha, the female energy of God, and how they expand. Krishna's first expansion was Balarama—the force of creation.

In my next dream, I met Balarama.

"Are you God?" I asked, overwhelmed.

"No," he responded.

"Is Krishna God?"

"Absolutely beyond a shadow of any doubt."

I woke up immediately afterward.

Doubt left me forever from that moment, but all the same, a later experience confirmed this new knowledge. This time, Lila and I were visiting a Self-Realization Fellowship temple in Yogananda's Church of All Religions. The monk who gave the sermon was greeting people afterward, and Lila suggested we go up and meet him.

Krishna and Radha by Vrindavan Das

His name was Brother Bimalananda. He was in his seventies
or eighties, meaning he'd actually spent time with Yogananda
in this life.

"Who did Yogananda say Jesus was?" Lila asked him.

"The Divine," he responded.

"But who did he say he was?" she prodded.

The monk walked us away from the others. "Yogananda said

Christ Jesus is Jiva Mukta, the son of God who is 'liberated while in the body,'" he told us in a low voice.

"Who did Yogananda say Krishna was?" I asked.

"Yogananda said Krishna is *Param Mukta*—'the supreme.' There's nobody higher," he explained. "But we don't teach that in the West. Yogananda was sent here to teach the love of God through the perspective of Christianity."

For most Christian people in America, Jesus is God, and Yogananda used that perspective to draw many closer to the ultimate truth. But I had had a wake up call, and I would never again deny that Krishna was the supreme God.

A SON AND A FATHER

The merging of my life with Lila's had profound effects upon other relationships in my life—old and new.

One such relationship was with my mom. My mother had always been relatively encouraging of my spiritual growth. When I told her about my dreams with Jesus, for instance, instead of reacting with anger as you might expect a Jewish mother to do, she just looked at me and said, "How did you take birth in my family?"

This was quite the evolution from the woman who once beat me just for being polite with a missionary who asked me to recite some verses from the Bible.

When I returned from Canada, my mother was the one family member I told about my battles with Staz. After I was visited by Yogananda, my mom agreed to read *Autobiography of a Yogi*. I also convinced her to read *The Science of Self-Realization* by A.C. Bhaktivedanta Swami.

Things became more complicated, however, after I introduced her to Lila. My mother really liked her, but she didn't trust the Hare Krishnas. She even went so far as to threaten to disown me if I joined that group. Like me, she admired Prabhupada, but she felt the organization that had grown out of his ideas was corrupt. And she had reason to be distrustful. One of her best friends had rescued her daughter from a Christian cult. She was scared something similar would happen if I grew too close to the Hare Krishnas.

More than anything, she was acting out of fear—I certainly had no plans of becoming a Hare Krishna—but her rebuke toward the woman I loved made me intensely angry just the same. I became so upset, in fact, that one night during a dream where my mother and I were arguing, I grew so angry in my sleep that I ejaculated. Sexual energy is a powerful force, and this was my body's response to the emotions that had been building in me toward my mother. It certainly placed a wedge between us.

There was also a new complicated relationship in my life: the one with Lila's son, Rama. Rama was extremely headstrong. His biological father, Srinivas, had not been involved in his life much—and only drifted further away after the divorce. So Rama wasn't used to having a strong male figure around.

From very early on in my and Lila's relationship, Rama saw me as his father. I still today refer to Rama as my son. I, too, even with such a poor relationship with my own father, still longed for that connection. But I told him to give me another name because I knew, at some point, he'd want his father in his life. So Rama began calling me Bapu, an affectionate Sanskrit term for father, and I began to take on that role.

Rama had been born into the Hare Krishna movement, but spending time with me opened his eyes to new ideas. One day, we were walking down the beach, and Rama saw a man catching a fish. Just as the fisherman reeled in the fish, Rama ran up to him: "He's still alive! You should put him back. He wants to live just like you do!"

Rama squatted down to get a closer look at the fish at the end of the fishing line. He'd been raised vegetarian and nonviolent, and everything he was saying was completely true.

I was moved, and so was the big, burly fisherman. The man bent down to come face to face with Rama, and explained that this fish was his dinner. This was a new outlook for Rama. We often shared illuminating moments like that whenever we spent time together.

LEAVING LAGUNA

It didn't take long before living in Laguna Beach became unbearable. It was so crowded all the time, and every time I'd sit in traffic to travel just a few miles, I was reminded of my dream of the mass exodus leaving Los Angeles and people not getting out in time.

We decided to move further north in California, to an area near Sequoia where Rama would go to school with other Hare Krishna children. Whenever we visited the school, Lila went in and spoke to the teachers, while I sat in the car with Rama and, sometimes, his friends.

One day, one of Rama's friends asked who I was.

"This is Mark," Rama said. "He's a Christian!"

That friend, not even bothering to open the door, jumped out the window. As a Hare Krishna, a Christian was just about his greatest fear. He'd probably have preferred if I was a serial killer. Rama just laughed and shrugged his shoulders, and I was thankful he was being raised with an openness others in his faith were not.

That openness was directly challenged by the school itself

when it started pushing for Rama to choose a guru. I vetoed the whole idea. I didn't trust the many self-proclaimed Hare Krishna gurus, so I suggested that Rama was old enough to choose his own, if so inclined.

"I can pick anyone?" he asked excitedly. Lila affirmed it.

"I pick Jesus," Rama said confidently.

Lila's mouth dropped. I just started to laugh. I didn't talk to Rama about Jesus much, but he knew my history and some of my experiences. I felt proud that he was making his own decisions and choosing his own path. Perhaps, also, that I was rubbing off on him.

My bonds with Rama and Lila were deep and growing deeper. But deep down, I also felt the itch to leave. My entrepreneurial aspirations were on my mind more and more, and while I advertised yoga classes, I didn't have a single client. We were living in Visalia, north of Bakersfield—a very conservative Christian area. No one in that community was interested in such things.

At the same time, I felt the need to run from the sense of attachment I felt growing toward Lila and Rama. I was bonding with Rama in ways I had never done with my own father, which I liked, but it also scared me. Lila, meanwhile, had begun to hint about getting married. Having grown up watching my own parents' dysfunctional marriage, that idea absolutely terrified me.

So I packed my bags and told Lila I was moving to the state at the center of my vision of the future: Oregon. She said she had to stay for Rama. The only way she could come is if I married her. It was the one thing I couldn't bring myself to do.

And so with a deep sense of conflict, I left. I thought I was saying goodbye forever.

PAST LIVES

For a number of years after Lila and I got together, people would sometimes stop us on the street to comment on the glow that seemed to be floating around us. "What do you guys do? You have this light around you," they would say. This was the power of love and the light of God. We were deeply in love, and others were able to see it and sometimes join us in this love. In Sanskrit, this type of love is referred to as Bhakti, and it comes in a variety of expressions. It would express itself in our relationship, our nurturing of Rama, and eventually in business.

Early on in our relationship, I used to ask at the end of my meditations how I could be so connected to Lila. It was explained to me once in a vision I had of us coming to Earth together:

> Lila and I are standing at the edge of another planet. We look at each other and say, "If you go, I'll go." We then take each others' hands and jump from the planet. We're flying through space, hand in hand. As we approach Earth, our hands separate, and our bodies drift apart. Lila floats off in the distance as she goes to take birth in Oregon, and I to take birth in Chicago.
>
> I crash into a vast body of water, sinking faster and deeper after such a great fall. And I keep trying to swim to the surface, but I can't. I just keep going down.
>
> "I'm drowning!" I yell. "I can't breathe! God, I'm going to drown; it's too deep!"
>
> Then I hear: "Just open your mouth, you can breathe."

I woke from that vision gasping for air.

The All Attractive Couple by Vishnudas (www.Krishnaland.com)

Once I got to Oregon, this vision was often on my mind. Despite my intent to break away, I missed Lila intensely. I realized I loved her immensely and needed her spiritually. After a very short period, I asked her to come be with me, and she made her expectations explicit: if she and Rama were coming, we'd have to get married.

I drove down to Northern California, packed up Rama and Lila, and took them with me. We were escaping California to settle in Oregon.

The apocalyptic era was still far in the future, but I knew it was certain to come eventually. After all, the rest of the dream had proven true.

LORD CHAITANYA

I am not a follower of the organization of Hare Krishnas, however, I recognize that the person who founded the movement is one of the greatest figures in history.

Lord Chaitanya Mahaprabhu started what we know as the Hare Krishna movement in India about 500 years ago, although he didn't call it that. The process was called Harinama Sankirtana, which is the practice of spreading the Universal message of Loving God by elevating society with ecstatic chanting and dancing.

Lord Chaitanya's message spread all over India. In his time, he defeated all of the Buddhist scholars, which was the other big movement going through the region at the time. He was known as a scholar at a very young age.

He started demonstrating miracles quite similarly to Jesus. He'd heal people, bring them back from the dead, cleanse lepers, and cast out demons. On one occasion, Lord Chaitanya put a mango seed in the ground, allowing it to grow before everyone's eyes. In fact, when I read about Lord Chaitanya, I was struck by how it was almost like reading the life of Jesus, except in a different time and part of the world.

Lord Chaitanya said he was opening up the storehouse of The Love of God and distributing it freely with the Holy Name to everyone. He'd offer food to God, and then distribute the remnants—blessed food—to the people, for free. I often found that when I'd go to the Hare Krishna temple, no matter how unsavory the food, I couldn't get enough.

"That's because the food offered is transcendental," Lila told me.

These acts were not done by an ordinary, devout man. Lord Chaitanya is the embodiment of Krishna and Radharani, Krishna's chief consort and the female energy of God. When you're chanting Hare Krishna, when you say "Hare," you're invoking Radharani. If you want something from your father, you go to your mother. So when you're chanting Hare Krishna, you're addressing both the male and female aspects of God.

Krishna is considered "all attractive." But Krishna is attracted to Radharani, so some people view her as even greater. Krishna even said he would come in the mood of Radharani to taste what she experiences. Reading the scriptures, you cannot deny that Lord Chaitanya is Krishna and Radharani in one body, just as Krishna said would happen. Lord Chaitanya also predicted that this movement he started would spread all over the world, and that is what Prabhupada helped make happen—even if the organization he left behind has sometimes fallen short and struggled to live up to his wisdom and devotion.

CHAPTER 7

NEW BATTLES AND NEW LOSSES

SETTLING INTO MY NEW HOME IN OREGON, IT SEEMED life was finally fully in order. I had love, a family, and a deep, rich spiritual connection that was stronger than ever. But as always in my life, the darkness returned and pulled me back into the pains of the material world.

In the first place, there was trouble with Ross. While living in Laguna Beach, Lila and I would often go on road trips to visit temples in Northern California. It was on one of these trips that I received a disturbing vision from Lila's guru about Ross.

We had checked into a Motel 6 and, as usual, I was sleeping on the floor. At 4 a.m. I felt Bhaktivedanta Swami's presence next to me. I sat bolt upright.

"Prabhupada was just here," I told Lila, alarmed. "He told me that Ross's thinking is all wrong, and we need to go back."

We immediately packed up our belongings and drove back to Los Angeles. I called Ross and asked him to come meet me at our parents' house.

"What's going on, Ross?" I asked, as he sat down at the kitchen table across from me and Lila.

"What do you mean?" he said. I knew he wasn't telling us something.

"Lila's guru came to me," I replied. "Something is wrong."

Ross started crying. "I'm thinking about killing myself," he confessed.

Consoling him, I told him, "If Lila's guru, whom you've never even heard about, cares about you, the world is bigger than you think."

Thankfully, that realization shifted his perspective, and he abandoned his plans. And for a time, he even embraced the spiritual lessons I'd learned and tried to apply them to his own life. He visited Yogananda's temples and read *Autobiography of a Yogi*. It would help for a short while, but Ross had been battling with darkness his whole life, and no matter how hard he tried, he seemed incapable of defeating the darkness for more than a season.

ROSS'S LIFE

Ross and I had always been close—although that didn't mean I was the ideal big brother. For a time, I hit him the way my parents and Martin hit me. Ross oftentimes was the recipient of my frustration. One day, Ross asked me why I was hitting him, to which I replied that I was only doing what was done to me. In Ross's innocent wisdom he replied, "Well, I have no one to beat up!" His words pierced my heart, and I apologized. I never again abused him in any way.

Ross always needed a little protection. He was so different from the rest of our family. He was the baby of the family, and he was always the most emotionally sensitive. He used to cry when Paul, Martin, and I were fighting. But, as I always told Dr. Bravin during my therapy sessions, Ross was the only person in my family who would joyfully hug me.

My mom told me once that she knew Ross was different even before he was born. She said that when she was pregnant with my older brothers and me, she knew we were boys. But when she carried Ross, it felt different.

Ross didn't look like the rest of us—he was softer than the rest of us, shorter, and lighter. He looked more like Mom, and had a perpetual twinkle in his eye like he was getting away with something. He also had a secret that separated him. I always knew Ross was gay, but the rest of my family never picked up on it. Perhaps they simply didn't pay enough attention to him.

Ross was eighteen when he asked me to be there so that he could "come out" to our parents. It was difficult for both Ross and our parents in the beginning. I was impressed when a week later my mother told me, "I don't know why I should care who Ross wants to love, that's none of my business. I am happy for him!" Our father, on the other hand, though he loved Ross, told me that he didn't understand Ross's choice. It was another point of tension between them.

Growing up gay and neglected in the '60s would have been hard enough, but Ross had other troubles too. Sometime during Ross's elementary school years, my mom was called in to talk to the principal. Ross was behind in school. He couldn't process ideas the same way the rest of us did. Likely, today he'd be diagnosed with ADHD or a similar learning disability, but back then, he was just "behind."

At the same time, Ross was creative in a way that simply wasn't accepted much back then. He enjoyed watching Ginger Rogers and Fred Astaire, and he loved Gene Kelly. He was also a talented artist who at an early age began trying to mimic masters like Marc Chagall.

Fiddler on the Roof by Ross Kenzer, age 9

Ross just seemed to process the world in a different way. Where my sensitivities turned me toward spiritual truth, his seemed to turn toward art and fantasy. And when the world didn't respond the way he wanted—when it rejected him or held him back for no other reason than who he was—he'd drift further into those fantasies to escape it.

Once, at the dinner table, my mother asked Ross about his

day at school. He told us a story about a kid who jumped up from his seat during class and said, "I'm late, I'm late for a very important date," before running out of the classroom. It seemed like something out of a cartoon, not a day in the life of a child. Later, we found out he'd seen the line in a commercial for Disney's *Alice in Wonderland*.

This distance between reality (material or spiritual) and fantasy only continued to grow. Into early adulthood, Ross had elegant tastes that couldn't match his bank account. He dreamed of being a star dressed to the nines and dancing on the stage—sophisticated, refined, and loved. He was always coming up with schemes to make that dream a reality. When he got his first car, he tricked out the Toyota mini pickup to look like a Mercedes. He tried to talk my mother, and later, my godmother, Ann Kay, into financing a restaurant. Then, he wanted to open a gay nightclub. But none of his ventures ever came to anything. After a number of setbacks, he stopped even trying. He began telling us that he was a makeup artist at Paramount, but we know that most certainly wasn't true. And he began stealing.

He even stole my mother's engagement ring.

He may have started stealing to buy some elegance, to fund the Liberace life he dreamed of, but eventually, it all went to buying the ultimate fuel of his fantasies—heroin.

Once Ross began using drugs, he headed downhill fast. My mother, however, couldn't face Ross's problems. She'd defend him, acting on her maternal instinct to protect, even when he caused her harm. I once discovered a bag of money in Ross's backseat—my mother's savings. When I tried to show her, she refused to look. She'd rather he take it than to see the truth.

After our conversation, Ross turned a corner. He entered a live-in detox program, and for about a year, he pulled himself together. He stopped using heroin and continued to embrace his new connection to spirituality. That year, Lila and I moved to Oregon, and once we were settled, I offered for Ross to move in with us.

Soon, though, I suspected he'd relapsed. I would invite him to join us for chanting, but he wouldn't wake up. He would then disappear late into the evenings. To protect Rama, I told Ross he had to move out. After that, signs of drug use continued. He would never answer his door or the phone. It would take a week for him to respond to a message. Soon, he moved back to Los Angeles.

One day, during one of my meditations, I had a vision that Ross had a gun. I called my mother.

My mom called me back and told me she had gotten the gun off of Ross, and he had confessed that he was planning to kill himself again. Crisis averted. But this time there was less respite. The end was near.

Not too long after that, I came to work and was told my mother had called and I was to call her back. Before doing anything, I turned to Lila and said, "She's going to tell me Ross is dead."

It was a prophecy I dearly wish had proven untrue. But my intuition was correct. Ross had overdosed.

He had been living in a rental that belonged to my parents, and when Paul found him, he'd been dead for ten days. His body was rigid, and his head was swollen. It was a gruesome scene for everyone. But when my mom arrived, she cradled Ross's head in her lap and wept for her poor baby boy. When I got to LA, she was still sobbing.

"I can't take it. I can't hold on," she cried. "I won't survive this."
I would soon find out she meant it.

LOSSES ADDING UP

I was no stranger to death by the time Ross died in 1991.

In my mid-twenties, I lost my old friend, Bob, my daily walking companion to high school and my garage bandmate. We'd drifted apart when our band broke up after high school, simply because we were in different places in life: I was exploring my spirituality and Bob was crafting a career as a brilliant musician.

Things had also ended quite awkwardly for me and Bob's sister, Pat, whom I had secretly dated in high school after we struck up our friendship. After high school, Pat and I had traveled to Great Britain together, but the relationship was never much more than casual to me. When I broke up with her, she was so hurt, she stalked me for a while. Later, she'd grow close to Paul, but she always avoided me from then on.

The year before I met Lila, Steve, the guitar player from our garage band, called me up and told me Bob had shot himself with his shotgun and was dead. I was devastated—my time with Bob was one of my few fond memories from adolescence.

At the funeral, I received an automatic writing about Bob that I read to his parents. It communicated that he was sorry for what he did, that he thought taking his life would change things, but it hadn't. He was still him, so he was going to work on himself now and move on. It was painful to hear this, but it helped them bring closure to the tragic situation.

In addition to the loss of Bob, my grandmother also passed on in the years leading up to Ross's death. It was around this time that, when I meditated, I found that I could communicate with the dead.

I'd done it with my grandfather—my father's father—when he had died. In his typical, rugged ability to take on anything, he had quickly accepted his death and told me he was waiting for me and my father. He further told me that he had a place for us.

So when my mother called me and said, "Bub (short for Bubbe, Jewish for grandmother) died," I immediately responded with, "Let me go find her."

I got off the phone and began to meditate. It didn't take me long to find my grandmother. I tried to talk to her, to help her through her bardo state and move on, but she wouldn't do it. Her lack of receptivity was frustrating to me.

I called Mom back and told her what happened. She just laughed.

"That's Bub. She never listens to anyone," she said.

Some time later, my grandmother came to me. "I'm so afraid," she said. "I'm just in darkness, and I wish that I had something like you."

I tried to help her find light. I told her to seek out someone she was familiar with, perhaps Moses, to elevate her into the next life. And for some time after that, when I meditated, I always sent Bub positive energy. I even asked Yogananda to help her find peace. Eventually, she must have drifted into a deep, dreamless sleep and taken birth again, as all who are lost eventually do.

When Ross died, I searched for him, too, during my meditations, but I have never been able to find him. Perhaps it's reflective of how he lived in this life—not accepting of his reality and never quite able to move on to his next journey.

Years later, a woman named Danielle, who didn't even know that I had a brother named Ross, told me that Ross had come to her in a vision.

"Your brother says he needs to talk to you," she said. "But he can only come after midnight."

She told me that a woman of darkness was controlling him, and he couldn't get out.

I have continued to search for him in all the years since his death, but until recently, I had never been able to encounter Ross. It is only now, twenty-one years later, that I can finally feel Ross's presence in my life again.

GOODBYE, MOM

When Mom told me she couldn't take it, I knew we didn't have long. After Ross's death, she began to look so frail. She was giving up.

"You still have three sons," I told her in consolation.

"But he was my baby," she cried.

I looked ahead in my own consciousness. I could see she would leave her body soon.

A little more than a year later, I got a call from Paul, and then another call from my father. They both told me Mom was in the hospital. She'd had a stroke, and the doctors had induced a coma.

There were other signs that told me something like this would happen. Ten days before the stroke, my mom came to Lila in a dream. In the dream, my mom rang our doorbell. She had her bags packed.

"Where are you going?" Lila asked.

"I'm leaving," my mother replied.

"Where's Jerry?" Lila responded, referring to my father.

"I've left him behind," my mother told her, waving her hand behind her. "I'm off."

Then, Lila woke up.

Immediately after getting off the phone with my father and brother, I went outside and began to meditate. Right away, I saw her, my mother, wearing a white chiffon robe.

"I'm out of here, Mark," she confirmed. "Tell everyone that I love them, but I'm moving on."

We prayed together, and I watched her go. It was a very beautiful moment.

I called Paul and told him that I saw her leave but it'd take time for everyone else to see it, too.

When I got down to Los Angeles, I saw my father in deep pain. It was the first time I ever saw him cry like this. A few days went by as the doctors tried various things to bring Mom back. Finally, my father told me they were taking her off life support. The medical world finally understood what I had already known.

When it came time for Mom's funeral, Martin, Paul, Pat, and I missed the entire thing. My father had told us it was happening at the graveside, only for it to be moved inside of the chapel. Amidst his hurt, he had failed to convey the message.

"You told us the wrong location!" I remember saying when he asked why we showed up at the end of the service.

It was a serious blow for me. For a time in our lives, my mom and I were best friends. I'd seen her leave; I knew she was okay. But it was painful to know she wasn't with me in this material existence. It was also painful to watch my father struggle with his grief.

His struggle, I'd find out later, was not just grief, but guilt. Years after Mom's death, Paul told me that the day of Mom's stroke, he'd received a phone call with no one on the other end. He hung up, and the call came through again. He picked it up, and he could hear breathing. It was Mom.

He called her back.

"If there's something wrong, tap on the phone," he said. He heard a tap, tap, and immediately hung up and called our father, who was working in his workshop.

"Dad, something's wrong with Mom. I think she just had a stroke. You have to take her to the hospital immediately," Paul had pleaded. Paul lived forty-five minutes away and couldn't get there in time to do it himself.

But Dad didn't go.

Paul waited for five minutes and called the workshop again. Dad, once again, answered.

"I'm finishing stuff up. I'm going, don't worry about it," Dad said.

"She's going to die if you don't go!" Paul screamed furiously, jumping in his car to drive there himself.

Dad did eventually take her to the hospital. By the time he got her there, though, it was too late. Mom was beyond the point of saving. That's probably why Dad was so devastated. He knew what he did.

After the funeral, the three remaining Kenzer brothers gathered together. Martin was the one to broach the topic on our minds.

"Do you want to stay in touch?"

Yes, we were brothers, but we'd always communicated through our mother. Now that she wasn't there, we'd have to consciously decide to connect.

"I'd have to know what that means," Paul said.

"What do you mean?" Martin asked, bewildered. "Mom's not here, so we'd have to try to connect on our own."

Paul was still suspicious. "I'd have to think about it," he said.

Martin just sighed. "I think I got my answer," he said.

From then on, I shifted into my mom's role. These days, Paul and Martin communicate only through me. That was only natural. I had been the one she was closest to. And after Ross, I was the most sensitive.

And being sensitive, I can still feel the place my mother's presence has left in me. It still pains me to think about her, even today, as I write this. I miss her.

DEATH MEANS LIFE

I was obviously upset when these people in my life died, but I was aware of a deeper reality beyond the immediate reactions.

Everyone is afraid of death because we've all taken birth, and we all know life is a temporary thing. We fear death, and we all project a false reality. It starts with parents telling children not to worry about death. It won't be for a long time, we tell them. We tell them the same thing when they fear our death.

This is a very Western perspective. In India, the answer would be closer to reality. Yes, I will die.

Because really, *death is life*. And life, even through death, is continuous.

As Krishna said, *"Never was there a time when you and I did not exist nor all these Kings, nor in the future shall any of us cease to be. As the embodied soul continually passes in this body from boyhood to youth to old age. The soul similarly passes into a new body at death. The self-realized soul is not bewildered by such a change."* (Bg. 2:12–13).

This reality becomes all the more apparent as you wake up. You realize who you are outside of your identification with the body and even with the mind. The mind is a subtle sense. Intelligence is higher than the mind, and it's even more subtle. You have those things to use, but they are not who you are. The soul lies beyond all of these.

This does not remove suffering from the experience of death, though. In fact, with a more open consciousness, it can make the experience more intense. You can experience death across time. It can be tormenting to experience death and suffering not only for yourself or others alive in this moment but in many moments.

The only support is that you can provide comfort to those suffering. When you understand the reality of death, you can provide individuals comfort in the same way a child can take comfort from seeing you remain strong and confident going forward in adversity. Once you overcome the fear and torment, you can aid with love.

"Resist not evil," Jesus said. This all works through love, but you must experience all of the mental anguish to get beyond it. Only then can you provide comfort through love.

CHAPTER 8

PACIFIC SPIRIT

IN 1986, LILA AND I WERE LIVING IN PORTLAND. AT THE
time, we didn't have much real work. I'd buy and sell some items,
but I was still too blocked by my experience with my jewelry
business to build anything more significant.

It was something I felt guilty about, but I was too hurt to
do anything about it just yet. I still can see Lila standing in the
kitchen of our rented home—unfurnished, as we couldn't afford
any furniture. We were happy but purposeless, muddling along
through our days. It wasn't all joyful. Returning home one day,
I saw Lila standing in front of the refrigerator with the door
open. There were tears in her eyes. We didn't have any food.

It was around this time that my friend Jerry called. He was
still in New York and had a job with Riviera, a sunglasses and
hair accessories company that he had repped for a number of
years. The company needed help catching up on their order
fulfillment. In need of cash and with nothing else to do, Lila
and I flew out to help.

We didn't put much thought into the trip, but it would have

a profound effect upon my life, Lila's life, and hundreds of lives in Nepal—and many more lives around the world.

It all came about in one of those moments that could almost be accidental (though nothing, of course, was ever accidental in my life). I walked past a store and was captured by a yoga poster I saw hanging on the wall through the window. The store merchant told me he wasn't selling the poster anymore but suggested I contact the person who created it—Dharma Mittra. When I went to meet him, though, he also couldn't sell me the poster. He'd thrown them all out.

"I have another one that might interest you," he said. He pulled out a giant poster. It was five feet long by almost four feet wide, with 908 yoga postures on it. "I was going to throw these away, too."

"Don't throw them away," I said. An excitement filled within me that I hadn't felt in a long time.

"Maybe you could help me sell them?" Dharma suggested.

Suddenly, the long-dormant entrepreneurial spark inside me began to flicker.

"Let me see what I could do."

Lila and I had very little money, but I took what we had and made an agreement with Dharma. He'd sell me the posters at a modest profit, and I'd sell them wholesale to New Age shops and yoga studios. That day, I gave him all of my cash—$25 total—for the first five posters. I rolled them up and went back to Oregon.

Despite my pledge and my not-insignificant investment ($25 was a lot for us back then), I didn't have a plan yet. All I knew was that there was value in these posters if I could get them in front of the right people. But how to do that? These were the days before personal computers. To find an address or a phone number, you had to use the Yellow Pages. But I only had the Yellow Pages for the Portland area. So, I headed to the library. I scoured all the Yellow Pages for cities across the country, writing down the address and phone number of every yoga studio.

Then, I took a picture of the poster, made a Xerox copy of it, and reduced the size to fit on a standard eight-and-a-half-by-eleven-inch piece of paper. On the back, I wrote the price of the poster—just a bit more than I'd paid—and our contact information. Lila, Rama, and I folded each piece of paper up, stuffed it in an envelope, and addressed each envelope by hand. I was so invested in the process, it took some time before I realized what I had done: for the first time since I was twenty, I had started my own business.

Within days of sending out the mailings, I began getting calls from potential customers: "We got your flier, send us your catalog," they requested.

What catalog? Already, this was more complicated than I had anticipated. And it was only going to become more so. Marketing experts told me that we'd need more items to increase how much each customer purchased and our possibility of a return on our investment. Otherwise, we'd lose money on each purchase because of the advertising costs. My friend, Jeff, who was working in marketing at the time, advised me to raise my prices. People would be more interested if they perceived value in the items we sold.

Lila and I took both pieces of advice and ran with them, creating a new company we called Pacific Spirit.

From day one, it was a hit. No one was doing what we were doing, and before we knew it, there were demands for everything we could think to sell. I had finally arrived at my place in the business world.

MAJOR SUCCESS

At that time, New Age was not a major industry. As far as I'd seen, there were only the rare New Age bookstores in big cities. For someone like my dad, that was a sign that no one was interested—and therefore, there was no market.

"You're wasting your time, Mark," he would bark at me anytime I told him about what I was doing. "Nobody's going to buy this crap."

Even Jeff had his doubts. "Are you sure there's a market for this stuff?" he asked me once.

But their hesitancy ran in direct contrast to the orders coming in the mail. It turned out that there was robust demand for the goods we were selling. Yoga was still in its infancy, and whatever new products we offered seemed to hit the mark. We added items like tongue scrapers, a little massage ball called the Pain Eraser, and PETA products for animal lovers. We sold New Age music and sound tools. Of course, we had crystals, and we even created a crystal chakra bag that contained a colored stone for each chakra.

All of those products sold well.

There were very few places where you could find these things, making the mail order business model perfectly suited to provide the products our customers were seeking. Soon, our small, black-and-white fliers morphed into bigger fliers, then into an eight-page catalog. Eventually, it became an eighty-four-page, full-color catalog, distributed to up to 800,000 customers per month.

We'd go on to publish two main catalogs: *Whole Life Products*, which offered alternative health and wellness products, and *Mystic Trader*, which showcased imported esoteric goods. We also published spinoff catalogs specializing in specific product areas, such as gemstones and beads.

When we started Pacific Spirit, we had $300 to our company's name, which we used to print and mail those initial fliers. After a year, we made $25,000. The next year, it was $45,000, and then $125,000, and then $250,000. Within a few years, I'd realized my dream of creating a company that could bring in $1 million. We didn't stop there. In the end, we grossed nearly $10 million in annual sales—a pretty good return on an industry that barely existed at that time.

And to think: this all started in our basement. Eventually, we'd buy a farmhouse with two warehouses on the property to hold our inventory, as well as the property next door so we could house our imports in the barn. We also converted a large chicken coop into an office.

It wasn't all good fortune. A few years in, we lost the rights to Dharma's poster. Dharma had continued to ship me posters from New York to sell, but he couldn't keep up with the demand, so I started printing them myself. This reinvestment, however, slowed the company's growth, and I eventually fell behind in payments back to Dharma.

This was an error on my part, but one made between friends. All Dharma had to do was ask for the back payment, and I would have sent it to him.

But then Dharma got married, and his new wife didn't see things in such a friendly light. In fact, she sued me. The settlement meant I had to stop printing and selling the poster, and she went on to sell the rights elsewhere. It hurt. Dharma was one of the most famous yogis in the country at the time, largely thanks to my efforts. Just as painful was the loss of his friendship.

But it was just one disappointment at a time when the business was otherwise on the upswing. There would be more betrayals and hurdles as our business grew, but in those early years, my experience for the most part was one I was completely unfamiliar with: a sense of financial thriving.

FULFILLING A CHILD'S VISION

During Pacific Spirit's infancy, we made contacts with local artists and stocked their handmade items in our catalog. But we soon learned they couldn't keep up with the demand. For a time, we paid others to import items for us, but we still struggled to fill every order within a reasonable time.

In the mail order business, there's a rule of thumb for how you measure how your business is doing. A 2 percent return on a catalog means break even—that is, if two out of every hundred people who receive the catalog make a purchase, you'll cover your expenses and make a small profit. A 3 percent return makes you good money; 4 percent means you're rich; and at 5 percent, you can't keep up.

Sometimes, we had so much interest at Pacific Spirit, we'd get a *6 percent* return on our catalogs. It wasn't just the catalog either. Customers would take the catalog to stores, and those stores would contact us to sell our wares wholesale.

All of this signaled that we needed a better way to collect inventory. Instead of relying on others for the products we sold, we needed to source them ourselves.

In 1988, two years into Pacific Spirit, Lila and I bought tickets for a three-month trip to India, with the goal of finding local artists whose products we could import. Lila's sister, Lorrell, and Rama came with us. We left a good friend, Chuck Lathrop, in charge of the business, which at that time, was still being run from the basement of our home.

The trip was extremely ambitious. Despite business booming, most of our profit went back into the company. We didn't have a lot of extra cash flow yet. We were still in the early, growing pains stage of business development. So, we couldn't afford to fail.

Though the main reason for the trip was business, it wasn't the only reason. Though Lila had been to India once before—she'd gone with a group of Hare Krishnas to meet her guru, and she'd been initiated in the holy city of Vrindavan—my physical body had never been. Going was a chance to connect with my own gurus and the sages who guided me. It was a chance to take a spiritual pilgrimage. It was also a fulfillment of the prophecies I had as a child: the importer traveling to the sacred, ancient lands of India and beyond.

As our plane landed in Mumbai that night, I could tell just by looking out the window that we were in a different world. Little campfires lit up the runway, families huddled around them—they were living there, right on the edge of the airport.

We stepped out of the plane onto the tarmac and the tropical air felt heavy and balmy. Children grabbed at us, asking us for money and food. Taxi drivers hounded us, asking us where we were going. The experience was overwhelming.

We stayed one night in a dive hotel near Mumbai, then made our way to a Hare Krishna temple in Juhu Beach, where many Westerners visiting India stayed. As a means to blend our spiritual and financial purposes, we drew up a list of temples and holy places we wanted to visit. Those locations influenced our path through the country. As we visited these sites, we would meander through local markets and villages in search of merchants to partner with.

Very quickly, it became clear that following an itinerary and doing business were going to be much more difficult in India.

First, we struggled just getting around. English wasn't that prevalent in India back then, but everyone was eager to help because, as Amercians, they presumed we had some money. Taxi drivers would often pretend to understand what we were saying, only to drive us off to a colleague who could translate once we got in.

We also had trouble transporting items around India. We knew we needed a broker to help us ship the goods we found as we traveled. However, the broker we engaged (whose office was inside a shipping container of all places) told us that we couldn't ship products around India like we could in the United States. If we bought something, we'd have to lug it along with us everywhere we went. Setback number two.

The whole trip might have become a disaster if not for a fluke—an unplanned trip to a country none of us knew much about at all: Nepal.

GOING TO KATHMANDU

Lila bought tickets almost at random to go to a town in Nepal called Pokhara. None of our holy sites were in Nepal. In fact, I didn't even know where the country was. My only knowledge of Nepal came from a Bob Seger song that referenced the capital, Kathmandu. But Lila was confident it was the right move. She'd secured first-class luxury tickets on the bus with a single-night stay at a hotel. And we could use some luxury at that point. Given our experience so far, I was a little leery, but we decided to go anyway.

My instincts proved right. Our "luxury" trip to Nepal was no such thing. Instead of a fancy intercity bus like you might find in Europe, we got on a broken down city bus. Our luxury was getting a few of the only real seats on board. That part of the journey was more comfortable than our "hotel," which was just a warehouse outside the city.

"You sleep here, you sleep here," the so-called proprietor yelled as he pointed us to flat futons on the floor that were our beds. Dinner was a cup of dal and a piece of bread. The bathrooms were outhouses. He advised us to get up early the next morning to catch the next bus to Pokhara. If we didn't get that bus, there wouldn't be another.

On the bus, we found out the source of all this disruption. India and Nepal's relations had broken down, and this was the only bus driving between the two countries. It wasn't clear how long the border would remain open at all.

The journey, as you can imagine, was terrible. The bus stopped in villages along the way, picking up more and more passengers. Soon, there were more than a hundred riders crammed onto the bus, packed in like sardines. Many climbed up on top, where they held on for dear life. The driver traversed the Himalayas like a maniac, causing the people who were riding outside on the top, hanging on for dear life, to throw up as the bus swayed from side to side.

As afternoon faded to dusk, the bus ran out of gas, puttering to the side of the road. The bus driver walked off without any explanation. Some kids emerged from the hills who, amazingly, spoke enough English to tell us that the driver had left to get some gas from the closest town. It would soon be dark, so many of the passengers walked off into the hillside, while others started making camp. Eventually, the driver returned with a badly dented five-gallon gas can. When the driver returned, a companion of his held a lighter near the gas tank—their terrifying way of creating enough light to see where the driver was pouring the gas into the bus. We all hurriedly backed away. Luckily, he didn't blow us all up. We had just enough fuel to coast downhill into Pokhara.

Of course, our adventure didn't end there. Once we arrived

in Pokhara, we met a Tibetan couple who told us to get to Kathmandu as quickly as possible.

"Buy whatever wares you need here and get to that city," they told us urgently. "You don't want to get trapped here. We have nothing."

Because of Nepal's severed ties with India, and the fact they were landlocked, everything in these smaller villages was severely rationed. People waited in long lines just to get food or fuel. We bought a lot of products from the nice couple, and they helped us load them onto the next bus scheduled for Kathmandu. This one, thankfully, was much nicer.

Because Kathmandu was a large city, I instantly felt safer, and we went looking for one major item: a prayer wheel. These were potentially very popular items for Pacific Spirit, and a good supplier might also lead to other purchasing opportunities. As we searched, another idea occurred to me. The prices in the market here were so cheap, even compared to India. Imagine what they must be if we could work directly with these original artists.

I learned the Nepali words for prayer wheel and craftsman and asked at each stall where to find one—with no luck. It was painstakingly hot, and everyone in our group was getting exhausted.

As we expected, prayer wheels were available in the markets, but we didn't want to pick up a few items. We wanted to find the craftspeople who made them.

"Let me just ask one more person," I said, promising that after that we'd go back to our hotel to cool off.

The shop was called Praksh Foam, not particularly auspicious for spiritual products. The doorway was so low, I had to duck just to get in. I was so exhausted and thirsty, I couldn't even talk. The merchant and I just stared at each other. Finally, I told him what I was looking for.

He didn't say anything at first. He just tapped his lip, looking at me and thinking.

"Ok," he said in broken English. "I will help you."

He introduced himself as Nem Bir Shakya and said he was from the Shakyamuni clan, the same one as the Buddha. Like most Nepali men, Nem Bir was short and had no body fat. He had a thick head of dark hair, a round face with dark eyes and a cherub-like smile.

Mark and Nem Bir

"C'mon," he said, and led me through winding back alleys. Lila, Lorelle, and Rama followed.

"We don't even know this guy," a worried Lila whispered as we walked briskly through the city. "Where are we going?"

"I trust him," I told her. Something inside me was telling me it was ok. "Let's just see where he's taking us."

We followed Nem Bir and ended up in a courtyard with eight people working there—hammering metal and cutting wood. They were making prayer wheels. Nem Bir began speaking to the person in charge in Newari, a Sino-Tibetan language spoken by the indigenous Newar people of Nepal.

"He's asking me how much I want, but I told him to give you the best price," Nem Bir told me. "Because you are from America and we can build a lasting relationship together."

The price was very affordable. I placed an initial order for a hundred prayer wheels, and Nem Bir helped me gather everything for our first shipment. Over the next few days, I found out just how lucky I was to find Nem Bir. As the owner of a metal business, he knew all the craftspeople in the area and could help to connect me to artists for Pacific Spirit. He also believed deeply in building up his community and raising their quality of life. And he was a descendant of the Buddha. It was a perfect partnership.

SHRAPNEL IN THE MAIL

That partnership nearly ended in ruin before it began. Nem Bir insisted against my better judgment that the agent he chose for us knew the ropes and that the cargo was in good hands. I should have trusted my instincts.

A few days after we returned to Oregon, I got a call from United Airlines.

"Your shipment's in, do you want it?" the representative asked.

"What do you mean, 'do I want it?'" I asked.

"You better come here and see," the person said.

When I arrived, I saw what she meant. My shipment, containing all the wonderful products we'd gathered on our trip to India and Nepal, looked like shrapnel. Everything was ruined or missing. This was our whole life savings.

Once again, though, we had luck on our side. The agent at United handed me a claims form, checking off each and every box describing possible damage. Scratched, dented, missing, broken—on down the list.

"Here, just tell us what we owe you," he said. "Sorry about this."

I let Nem Bir know that we couldn't afford to make the trip again. He came to the rescue.

A month after the incident, he called me. He told me that I could stop working with my broker in India. He could help me directly if I could send him $250 to get started. I scraped up the cash and wired him the money.

He was as good as his word. Thanks to Nem Bir, Pacific Spirit became the largest importer from Nepal, and Nem Bir became the country's biggest exporter.

When the next shipment came in from Nepal, it was emotional for me. My vision as a child—that I would be a mystic, importing items from India and foreign lands—had truly become a reality.

"It's happening," I thought. "This is what I always thought I would be doing."

And soon I would discover all the good I could do in fulfilling that vision.

A BUSINESS THAT CHANGED LIVES

Lila and I would take several trips to India and Nepal as we grew Pacific Spirit. Not only were we business partners, inspired by our business and spirituality, but we were madly in love. It made the work fun, and for a while, life was really good.

On our second trip, we met up with Nem Bir again.

"Mark, come with me," he told me. "I want you to meet somebody."

Nem Bir took me to Lalitapur and introduced me to a man who spoke only Nepali. Nem Bir translated for me.

"Mark, this man has this land," he said pointing to the lot in front of us between two old buildings.

"He has always wanted to build a free health clinic for Nepal," Nem Bir said. Nem Bir explained that the Medicine Buddha, an image of a blue Buddha holding a pot of medicine, had appeared to the man. At the time, healthcare wasn't widely available in Nepal, and there were only a couple medical doctors in the whole country.

"Maybe you have some ideas for him," Nem Bir said.

They were only looking for advice, not money. The expectation was that I could offer ideas about how to make this clinic happen. Still, the seed was planted in my consciousness.

Later that day, Lila and I were in a store and saw this huge thangka, a type of Tibetan painting. It was eight feet long and four feet wide, showing a detailed depiction of the pastimes of Lord Buddha. I instantly fell in love with it.

The price tag was hefty for us, so I asked Nem Bir to negotiate for me. Nem Bir, too, agreed it was a high-quality painting, but the shopkeeper wouldn't budge on the price. Newly invested with higher profits from Pacific Spirit, I bought it anyway. I decided to take the thangka home, reduce the image down, and sell it as posters. All the money would go to Nem Bir to help him create this clinic.

Unfortunately, the posters didn't sell well. We were actually losing revenue simply having them in our catalog. I even put the original thangka in the catalog for the price I'd bought it for. No one bought it. I felt terrible. I hated that we didn't have the sales to help support Nem Bir's mission.

A year later, however, two days before our next trip to Nepal, I got a call. It was from a doctor in Minneapolis. He wanted to buy the thangka.

This was obviously amazing news, but I was on a tight timeline if I was going to make a present of that money to Nem Bir. I told the doctor I was going to Nepal in two days and asked if he could overnight me the money. He agreed. I couldn't be more excited that I would get to show up with cash in hand for the health clinic in Nepal.

When I arrived in Nepal, though, Nem Bir pulled me aside before I could share the news. He told me that *he* had a surprise for *me*.

"We've broken ground on the health clinic!" he announced.

"What?" I asked. "How are you doing that?"

"We don't have the money, but we know it will come," said Nem Bir confidently.

He wanted me to talk at a groundbreaking ceremony they were holding at the site of the new clinic.

"All the elders will be there," he said. "You talk; I'll translate."

Before we went, though, I had to share my surprise with Nem Bir.

"I'm happy to speak at the event and do whatever else you require of me. But Nem Bir, I have to tell you something wonderful. I have the money."

He blinked. "How much?" he asked.

"All of it."

It took him a minute to understand what I was saying. When he got it, he started dancing and tapping his lip.

"We'll just tell everyone that you are going to donate $500," he suggested. "If we say you have it all, no one will want to work. So, we will say you will donate more if we do good work."

So that's what we did. I gave $500 to get the health clinic started and said if they kept working, more money would come.

With $7,500 still in my pocket, Nem Bir took me to meet a woman. She and her husband had a vision to start an education foundation to educate and lift women out of poverty. The vast majority of women there couldn't read and write. They had no trade, so they couldn't earn money. This left them at the mercy of cruel men, stuck in violent marriages with no escape. So we decided to set up a school. The deal was we'd teach these women a trade if they agreed to learn how to read and write. Many of their crafts made their way into the Pacific Spirit catalogs. We fronted the materials, all they had to do was put it together, and they'd get paid. They'd also have an education and an independent income.

Women Cooperative, Mark (center rear, L), Pam (R), Nem Bir

In just the early days of the school's operation, we helped 300 women. They all now had the ability to leave if the men in their lives hurt them. They were no longer trapped. Many of them joined together and opened a gift store featuring their handicrafts.

The third charitable business we set up was a microbank. We found that there were many artists in Nepal, but they didn't have the money to buy their materials in bulk. They'd have to walk to Kathmandu just to buy a small amount, then walk all the way home, create their art, sell it, and walk back with the profits to buy more. They wasted days walking when they could be working and creating or at home caring for their families. With a loan of $10 to $20 from our microbank, they could buy far more material, work on more projects, save time, and get ahead.

Giving back and helping others is a mindset I have always had—thanks to the values my mother instilled in me as a child. I'm proud that my $7,500 painting was the start of something that changed hundreds, if not thousands, of people's lives. All three nonprofit businesses are still running today.

I applied that same mindset to my business back in America, too. I made a point of never turning down anyone who came to me for work. Many of the employees at Pacific Spirit were single women with large families to support.

When I hired them at Pacific Spirit, I told them the only expectation was that they showed up in the morning for work. Then, I started offering them hypnosis to treat some of their bad habits. Soon, many of the women stopped drinking and smoking. They were empowered to change their lives, just like the women in Nepal.

This is all beside the value we brought in introducing New Age ideas into America. Truly, we were on the cutting edge of providing spiritual nourishment throughout the country. Customers would buy earrings and pins with Sanskrit Om symbols without even knowing what they were. They were just drawn to them. I once received a call from someone who had a spontaneous cancer remission simply by seeing a poster of a thangka we printed in the catalog.

Pacific Spirit also produced millions of devotional and sacred images within the pages of its catalog that were distributed freely throughout the US, including representations of Christ, Krishna, Buddha, Rama, Radha, and Lakshmi, to name just a few.

These experiences made sense of my life of failure before. I couldn't have helped all these people if I had been a success selling jewelry or Victorian clothes or cookies on the streets of New York. If I'd gotten a "normal" job, none of this would be possible. This was what I was meant to do. Karmically, I was drawn to Pacific Spirit. This was the path reserved for me in this life.

It was the only explanation how a glimpse of a yoga poster in a city I didn't even live in led to a business, which led to a trip to a country I wasn't even meant to visit. And yet, when I got there, it felt like I was home. This is the impact I was meant to have in this current physical incarnation. This was my home.

THE NATURE OF SPIRITUAL PILGRIMAGE

When you're on a spiritual pilgrimage, it's amazing how things just open up for you. People you've never met guide you through difficulty, like they were placed there just to help you. Random events come to have profound meaning.

In this way, Nem Bir appeared and opened many paths for me through the spiritual journey of Pacific Spirit. But it happened in more minor ways on my first trip to India as well.

Lila, Lorrell, Rama, and I were in the Howrah railway station in Kolkata, one of the busiest stations in the world. We were completely overwhelmed. We wanted to visit the ashram of Yogananda's guru in Serampore, but we had no idea how to get there—or how to even get tickets.

The station was packed, with tens of thousands of people going in and out nonstop. We couldn't get to the ticket counter. Women were allowed to go to the front of the line, but men would push forward, cutting in front of them. The four of us held hands as we made our way through the crowd, trying to figure out where to go and what to do, all while making sure none of us got lost.

Then, a twelve-year-old boy approached us.

"Can I help you? Where are you trying to go?" he asked, in fluent English. I told him our destination.

"I can help you," he said. "How many tickets do you need?" He held out his hand and in it, I placed the money for four tickets to Serampore.

Then, he disappeared into the crowd. I wasn't sure where he went, but as with Nem Bir, I felt I could trust him. Fifteen minutes later, he showed up again.

"Come on," he said, "I've got your tickets. I'm going the same way and will go with you."

When we got to Serampore, the boy put us on a bullock cart. He translated for us to the driver so we got where we wanted to go, and we enjoyed a full pilgrimage at the ashram.

As our next train rolled into the station, there was the same boy again. He asked where we wanted to go. We were headed to a second temple, the Kalighat Temple, and he took us there, too. Then he rode back with us to Kolkata. He asked for no payment and no prize for all his kindness. His path simply mysteriously always followed ours, and he was always able to guide when we needed it most.

This is the nature of spiritual pilgrimage. You feel the hand of God making everything happen for you. It's remarkable, enlightening, and eye opening.

Sometimes, however, the events of a pilgrimage can open your eyes to things you don't want to see. On another trip, we were in a room on the tenth floor of a building. A bee flew into the room and stung Lila on her wedding ring finger. Bees aren't meant to fly that high. I'm not sure how this bee even did that. But, Lila is allergic to bees, and due to the sting, her finger swelled and her ring had to be cut off. This, it turned out, was a sign of what was to come.

CHAPTER 9

THE HEART OF THE MATTER

HE'S GOING TO DIE.

These words may have been the first words I heard when I entered this world as an infant, when the doctor told my mother how ill I was. And throughout my life, I have had this foreboding feeling that the doctor was right—that something was wrong with me, and I wouldn't last a normal lifespan. I was on borrowed time. It instilled an unconscious fear in me.

For years, I didn't acknowledge or comprehend that I had this fear within me. It was simply something that lingered at the back of my mind and in my dreams. Soon, it would force itself to the front of my consciousness.

Within a few years, Pacific Spirit was still doing well, and we had become a multimillion-dollar corporation. Having achieved my goal as a child to make a million dollars, I now felt like I was at a crossroads. Our business was asking more of me than I could give emotionally, mentally, and physically. My stress levels were high. And I felt less motivated to suffer the stress and meet those demands. I had cleared my entrepreneurial karma.

But at the same time, I wasn't willing to walk away from it just yet. Lila and I had spent years building Pacific Spirit. Now, many people depended on us. There were the workers in Nepal, our team in Oregon, and all of our customers. How could I walk away from all those people simply because the stress was high?

But the stress was getting higher—so high, in fact, that Lila suggested that we simply close the business. "Let's just shuffle the deck and see how the cards fall," she said.

We didn't close, and things got worse. We were having an issue with an employee, Gail, our warehouse manager, whom we'd hired and let live in a guest house on our property. Gail was going out of her way to try and come between Lila and me. Her efforts were so intense, I dreamed that Gail crawled into bed and forced her way between Lila and me. This couldn't continue, and Lila and I knew we had to let her go.

The day we decided to do it, Lila and I were also going to sign papers to place an offer on a house that was a fifteen-minute drive from the business. Up until this time, our home was on the same land as our business, and our employees had access to us whenever they wanted. This new house would allow us to keep our work and home lives more separate.

That afternoon, we confronted Gail and told her she would no longer be working at Pacific Spirit and she needed to move out as soon as she could find a new place to live.

It was a hard conversation, and immediately after, I paid for it. As we got in the car to meet our realtor, I noticed my heart was beating quite fast. So fast, in fact, that I became dizzy and almost fainted.

I had experienced this same lightheaded dizziness on a few other occasions, but I never let Lila know about them. I would just wait until the symptoms passed and continue going about my business. But this time, my heart's erratic behavior wasn't ending as quickly as it usually did.

"Lila, my heart is racing. I can't slow it down," I said as we sat in the driveway. We sat there for another ten minutes. It was still racing. I tried running it off, but it put too much pressure on my heart.

"Lila, I think I must be having a heart attack," I said.

My heart was now doing close to two hundred beats per minute. I tried to meditate, that always calmed me down. It helped a little, but my heart's thumping remained relentless.

He's going to die.

The words rang in my mind. I called my father and brothers to say goodbye, but no one answered. I went outside to sit behind a warehouse. If I was going to die, at least I could do it enjoying the lovely view provided by the twenty-eight acres our home and business sat on.

I started to cry uncontrollably.

"Lila, you must let me go. I can't take this anymore," I felt terrible saying these words, projecting my fear and pain onto the only person I ever truly loved.

"Mark, I'm not stopping you if this is what you want," said Lila, sounding scared and sad.

But then, I changed my mind. I had a dim sense that my journey in this life was not yet complete. "No, please take me to the hospital," I said.

"And tell the realtor I'm sorry we won't make our appointment."

That's Mark Kenzer: considerate to a fault, even when he's having a heart attack.

At the hospital, I was rushed into the emergency room and hooked up to a number of machines. Over the beats of various devices and the strong smell of disinfectant, the doctor on call started his intake.

"When did this start?" he asked.

"About two hours ago." Lila replied.

"I would like him to answer," he said harshly.

He continued down his laundry list of questions.

"Do you drink coffee or soda? Have you taken any medications or drugs of any kind? Do you smoke? Did you just eat Chinese food?"

I answered no to them all as my arm and throat began to tighten. My heart was now doing 245 beats per minute.

I felt very lightheaded, like I was going to pass out. The doctor then asked me to tense my body and release it. Nothing happened. He tried rubbing my carotid artery. Nothing changed. Then, he asked the nurse to get an injection.

"My friend, you are having a heart attack," the doctor said. "This will stop it."

The nurse put a needle in my vein, and the doctor gave the order. My heart came to an abrupt halt, flatlined for a few seconds, and then regained a somewhat-normal rhythm.

I started to cry either from the dose of adrenaline or the sudden drop in blood pressure. I just about passed out but slowly made my way back. Tears were in Lila's eyes as she held my hand.

"I'm glad that you didn't go. I didn't know what I'd do without you," she said.

Our moment of gratitude and calm was short lived. As I regained clear consciousness, the nurse pulled Lila aside and told her I had not, in fact, had a heart attack. They weren't sure what had happened or when it would happen again.

Whatever my future and however much of it I had, I wanted to go home. Lila asked the doctor if I could leave.

"You're not going anywhere," he said.

"He just had a heart attack," he yelled at Lila. "Do you want him to die?"

He turned to me, his face twisting in anger, his voice rising, "If you leave, you'll die, I guarantee it."

He's going to die.

The words from my childhood flashed before me again, and this time reconfirmed by another doctor four decades later.

After much argument with the doctor, I was finally allowed to unhook myself and go to the bathroom. Alone with myself, I prayed to Yogananda. He gave me simple instructions: "Get out, just get out."

When I came out of the bathroom, I caught Lila's eye. She asked me what Yogananda had said. She knew me well enough to know what I had been doing.

"Ok then, let's go," she said without hesitation.

I told the doctor I was leaving and he exploded in anger. His face turned red as he screamed, "You'll die! I promise you'll die!" He paced the aisles between the beds. I looked at the nurse and she just shook her head.

I signed a release form and Lila helped me outside. Once there, I sat on the grass and cried, breathing in the fresh air. If I was going to die, at least it would be surrounded by nature and not with that man shouting in my ear.

When we got home, I just lay on the couch until evening came. Despite my escape, the doctor's voice still rang in my ears. You're going to die. I promise, you will die.

I couldn't get rid of that voice. It kept me awake for many, many nights.

ISSUES OF THE HEART

I had long had issues with my heart, although I hadn't really examined them. There were the problems I experienced as a young man when my jewelry business dissolved and life seemingly fell apart. Sandy had helped see me through those.

In Toronto, I felt the war wounds of my battle with Staz directly in my heart. When she disappeared from my life, though, so did the pain. When Lila would spoon me, I would move her hand away from my heart. But so long as she kept her hand from that location, I could ignore that discomfort.

Throughout my life, my heart was always where I felt most vulnerable and where the pain of my spiritual encounters resided. But for this precise reason, I was reluctant to fully examine this pain.

After my first flatlining in the emergency room, though, I had no choice. It was time to find out at least what the material, medical reason was for my current pain.

I called my brother, Paul, who also told me I had not had a heart attack. He knew because he had the same condition—a type of arrhythmia—which he'd had for several years. His condition was not as severe as mine—he had always been able to bring his heart rate back down on his own—but the symptoms were unmistakably the same. A few days later, I went for a number of tests, which confirmed what my brother suspected.

But why was this happening to me? How could I, of all people, have a heart condition in my forties? I had no bad habits; I was vegetarian; I meditated.

It was only later that I realized that my heart issues came from my fear. They were not old friends on the same path, they were one and the same. And, in fact, the fear was not my own. When I had heard the words *"he's going to die"* as a newborn, they had been said not to me but to my mother. This was my mother's fear.

From the day I was born with such difficulties, my mother feared I wouldn't make it. As a child, while I was the one living with boils and nightmares, she had to watch helplessly as I suffered. Despite her faults as a mother, her maternal love was strong; it had killed her when Ross died.

And that love—and fear—had transferred to me.

How much she must have suffered watching me suffer. It was only natural that some of that carried on in my life. Her fear literally weighed upon my heart.

So while the pain in my heart and the fear remained, it was in some sense a gift—because it was an inheritance from her.

THE LOST CHILD

I was well-acquainted with the fear of parenthood from my role as a father to Rama, but I would soon also learn the pain of loss.

Often, after my regular meditation periods and daily Kriya yoga practice, I would sit and listen, basking in the after effects of my exercises before starting my day.

One morning, I heard a voice from far beyond making its way into my consciousness.

"I want to ask you something," it said. "I was hoping you could help me. I need to take birth. This should be my last time; I died before I could finish. And if you and your wife could be so kind, I would be very grateful."

Her presence was unlike the others who had come to me during my meditations. Her vibration was very lofty, like someone with a deep realization and practice.

We spoke briefly. I told her that I understood her dilemma, having only recently contemplated my own fate if my life was cut short. However, it was never my intention to have children. Rama was my son, but I had not brought him into the world and did not intend to bring another in now. After my own childhood of illness in a very dysfunctional and abusive family, I could never justify introducing a new life to such circumstances— even if Lila and I had never behaved as our own parents had.

But the voice persisted, visiting me again the following day. I told her that I would think about it and discuss it with my wife.

Lila had always wanted to have at least one other child. It had only been my own fears of replicating my parents' behavior that stopped us. And no amount of years of love and connection with Rama could ever convince me entirely that I could rise to the occasion.

What if my child was like me, with health issues and spiritual sensitivities? What if, having brought a child into life, I some- how fell into the old habits of my parents that I had avoided with Rama? I reasoned it was better to not even consider the idea.

But now I was being pushed. I knew what Lila would say, and now another soul needed my help. Was I really going to consider this?

To my surprise, the more I sat with it, the more that it seemed to be an ok idea. Whoever the soul was, they had made a lot more progress than I had. They should be a breeze to raise compared to what I was used to.

I spoke to Lila about it.

"Someone wants to take birth in our family," I told her. "She's a very advanced yogini (a female yogi). She says she needs to take just one more birth and wants to know if we would help her."

Lila's surprise even exceeded my own. She couldn't believe I was even considering this, but she agreed. And so we increased our spiritual practice and then chose the day to conceive. On that day, we meditated together and invited this person into our lives.

At the moment of conception, there was an inner burst of light. Lila could see and feel it, too. Immediately, things became much different. There was a new light in our house.

For me, the thought of raising the yogini took on a new meaning. Since conception, we had continued to meet through our consciousnesses. Not just during daily meditations but also in most of my waking hours and even sometimes while sleeping, my new daughter and I had loving exchanges.

Lila also took on a new glow. After we told Rama, the whole family was excited, though we decided to wait some time before sharing the news with others.

Lila was about two months pregnant when everything fell apart. One day, I was sitting in my usual meditation when my little yogini came to say goodbye.

"I want to thank you," she said. "I am leaving. I have completed what I needed to and now I'm moving on."

"What?" I was taken aback. Though I knew that I should be happy for her and celebrate this moment, I couldn't help but feel despair. I had become very fond of the idea of having a child. But the yogini was gone as quickly and silently as she had come.

I didn't know what to say or how to tell Lila, or even if that was a good idea. As evening approached, Lila became uneasy. She was experiencing some pain and feared something was wrong. I feared not telling her what I knew, but I also feared telling her. What if it wasn't true?

Soon, her pain began to worsen. She went into the bathroom, and I laid down on the floor, a few feet from the closed door.

The heaviness taking over me was almost too much to bear.

I could hear Lila crying out. She was bleeding. I was slowly becoming unconscious. This was all happening too quickly, but it was happening just like the yogini said it would. She was gone, and Lila was left with the pain and sorrow of having lost her baby.

That night, I told Lila what I had known and explained I couldn't be sure and was afraid to say anything. I thought I was doing the right thing, and Lila did, too.

This became a great lesson for me that not everything sweet turns to nectar. And no matter the length of our timeline, death always has its way with us.

And in the wake of that death, there is immense pain for all who remain.

NEW COMPANIONS

With everything going on in my life at this time, I found comfort and friendship in a familiar place: the animals in my life. My relationships with my dog, Bhima, and my horse, Lucifer, taught me more about my material and spiritual worlds than I ever thought possible, and they left profound and lasting imprints on my life.

Bhima came into our home at about seven-and-a-half weeks of age. Lila saw a classified ad in the *Oregonian* offering shepherd-malamute mix puppies for only $10. It ended up being one of the best investments of our lives.

Although I shouldn't overattribute our part in joining Bhima to our family. The truth is that Bhima chose us. As I entered the garage of the man who advertised the puppies, eight adorable little fur balls surrounded me. I stood in the middle, grabbing them as they ran around, looking for a female to take home.

The first dog to come directly to me sat at my feet and looked up at me. I picked him up and noticed that he was a male. Back he went. I picked up another, also male. Each time after that, when I picked up a puppy, it was male. It didn't take me long to realize that I was looking at the same dog. Every time I put him down, I watched as he ran back into the pack and then ran in front of me again so I'd pick him up. After about the fourth time, I went back out to the car, where Lila and Rama were waiting.

"There's a male who really wants to go home with us," I told them. "Is that ok?"

Bhima made sure he was the dog we took with us that day. It wasn't long before we realized that this wasn't a fluke—that Bhima was no ordinary pup.

He was easy to train, almost as if these were easy tasks to master for one so wise in the world as he. We noticed early that Bhima adopted many of our habits and followed them loyally. Though we offered him meat, very early on, Bhima insisted on being vegetarian with the whole family. Moreover, he refused to let anyone who ate meat come close to him. He could sense if someone ate meat, and he'd growl anytime they approached. He also refused to eat on Mondays, the same day Lila, Rama, and I fasted to cleanse our bodies.

As he integrated into our family, Bhima took on more of our spiritual practices. For instance, every morning, we would gather together in our temple room to read, meditate, and have kirtan, which is devotional singing. Bhima would join us on most mornings and would even offer his obeisances, lowering himself on his front legs, and placing his head on the floor in front of the altar. He didn't always sit still, but he never once disturbed any items on the altar. Sometimes, he would join us in singing.

Bhima and I bonded in a way I'd never had with another animal. We shared a psychic connection.

When Bhima was home alone, I could receive mental images from him of what had happened in or around our home. When

I walked in the door, I would lower my head to receive Bhima's greetings, and he would whisper licks in my ear about events that had occurred.

Many times, he would tell me someone had called, and this would be confirmed by a message left on our answering machine. When he told me who had come to the door, we would call that person to find out why they had stopped by.

As Bhima continued to display his unique behaviors, the thought that he may have been a human in his past life began to cross my mind. How many dogs were vegetarians or went to temple each day and bowed down before the altar?

One morning, I even caught Bhima worshiping a life-size wooden goddess of a seated Kwan Yin that was in our living room. As he passed her, I watched as Bhima stopped to give her a kiss. Very gently, he gave her face a few licks and then walked into the kitchen to lie down. I later discovered that he would sleep with his head in her lap when we were away. Obviously, this wooden carving did not have a human sense, but Bhima loved her just as any devotee may become attracted to an image of Christ or Buddha.

Bhima wasn't the only animal friendship in my life in these years. There was also a horse. When I would tell people that the name of my horse was Lucifer, they would often act surprised: "Why don't you change the name?" they'd ask. Why would I do that? Lucifer is from the word *luce* and refers to light. And despite his brusk exterior and dark coloring, my Lucifer definitely had a spirit of light. And if I had judged him by his name, I would never have learned how to see past many of my own shortcomings.

Mark and Lucifer

I purchased Lucifer from a woman named Ruth. She not only trained Lucifer but helped to train me as well.

"This horse is going to teach you the lessons you need to learn in your own life," Ruth told me. "And one lesson you need quick is that you're not taking the reins in your own life."

This was true in my business, and even in my relationship with Lila. I often let things slide due to fear of asking for what I truly wanted. Riding Lucifer taught me how to finally overcome this—how to take control of my situation and ask for what I wanted. It was a lesson that would guide me in the years ahead, after my second dark night of the soul.

Before Lucifer's wisdom would help me in my darkest days, though, I had much else to learn. In the first place, I had to learn how to ride a powerful, bold, and stubborn animal like Lucifer. I had been taking riding lessons for some time when Ruth had asked me if I wanted to ride him. I was excited and nervous. This was Ruth's own horse, a proud, powerful animal whom she took to Nationals and won.

Before learning to ride with Ruth, I had always been very hesitant around horses. The few times I'd try to ride, as soon as I was on a horse, the fear would overcome me and I would jump off. Often, when Lila would take her riding lessons, she would encourage me to come along and try to ride, but I'd end up just sitting in the car watching. With Ruth, I'd improved, but I was still taking lessons on a very gentle, cooperative horse. Riding Lucifer was entirely different.

This fear came from a past life. Years earlier, I had seen my own death happen on a horse. On the day of that vision, I had gone with Lila to look at a horse she was considering buying. As she spoke with the man selling the horse and rode off on it, I sat on the truck gate, waiting. I closed my eyes and soon entered a trance-like state. I saw a horse running full-gallop through desert-like plains. I noticed a Victorian-age dress blowing in the wind, worn by a woman riding the horse sidesaddle. The woman, I realized, was *me*.

It was like one of those dreams where you are watching yourself from above. I watched, my heart racing, as the woman and her horse ran full speed until they reached the edge of a high, steep cliff. The woman tried to stop the horse, but it was too late—the horse's hooves slid over the cliff and they both tumbled down. The woman smashed her head on a rock and that was it. She—*I*—was dead.

No wonder I had always had so much interest in Victorian clothing. No wonder I had been gripped with fear before I could open a Victorian clothing shop. After this experience, though, about 95 percent of my fear was completely gone. I figured the remaining 5 percent was for my own safety and the reverence and respect that should be shown to any animal.

So you can imagine my apprehension getting on a horse who set out to test my control. But that's who Lucifer was, and that's what I did. When I'd put the bit near Lucifer's mouth, he'd grab it from me because he wanted to take charge. Whenever I picked up the reins, he'd grab them back.

When I'd hesitate, Ruth would chide me. "Are you riding him or is he taking you for a ride?" she would say. "You better take control or he's going to. Only one of you can be in charge."

Over time, my confidence riding Lucifer grew. Finally, Ruth asked if I'd like to buy Lucifer. It was a lot of money, but I didn't hesitate. Lucifer was meant to be in my life forever.

Still, there were certainly times when I wanted to give Lucifer back. As he settled in at our home, he continued to find ways to test my authority. I had to learn the cues that would tell him what I wanted and where I wanted to go. Riding Lucifer was like riding on top of a living sports car, but I had to find the boldness to tell this thousand-pound creature that I would be making the decisions.

For a time, Lucifer would make me chase after him if I wanted to ride. He'd run away and dodge me, and it'd take fifteen minutes to catch him. One time, I got annoyed and I gave up on him. I said in frustration, "Lucifer, you're an asshole." When he saw me get another horse, he whinnied in protest.

That night, he came to me in a dream: "I am not an asshole," he said. "I am a horse. And I'm doing what horses do."

His wisdom, like Bhima's, was deep and ancient. He was right, of course. I realized I wanted him to be the horse that he was meant to be, not the one who I had to change to fit my own fears. He had to make me chase him because he had to prove his dominance to the other horses. That was part of who he was. A creature must be what it is. If I was here to fulfill my own part in existence, so was Lucifer—even if his part sometimes annoyed me. Once I understood what he was feeling, I stopped making it a big deal. And from then on, he rarely ran far from me, even with the other horses watching. When I rode him, he always performed as best he could.

Lucifer taught me more than how to ride. Through him, I learned how to live, to love, and to guide—all things I'm hoping shine through in this book, as well. Handling a horse takes practice, and learning to connect takes love. You have to let them have their own energy and redirect them when needed in a loving way. That's true of people as well. You can't force someone to be something they're not, all you can do is love and guide them. Ultimately, they'll choose their own path.

CONTINUED HEART TROUBLES

Despite these fulfilling and close connections with Bhima and Lucifer, I was still haunted by the pains of my heart—the physical pain of my arrhythmia and the emotional pain of losing the yogini. I could hear the voices of those two doctors in my ear: the first at my birth (*he's going to die*) and the other confirming in the hospital (*you'll die*). My fear—the fear I'd inherited from my mother—made me cautious about everything I did, even when things went perfectly fine.

When Lila and I traveled to New Zealand, for instance, it was fantastic. But throughout the trip, my worry never escaped me. During the flight, I wondered what would happen if my heart rate increased dramatically while we were over the ocean. I could die.

We went black water rafting and I loved it, except for the fact that we were underground for over an hour and I was afraid that my heart could explode at any moment.

And the arrhythmia did continue. One year after that first

episode, my heart started to race just as it had before. Thankfully, the doctor in this emergency room was great, and gave me the same treatment the first doctor had, only he didn't shout prophecies about my early demise.

He told me to follow up with a specialist, but I didn't. I had a deep distrust of most medical practices, and perhaps I was simply unable to face my fear directly. Instead, I chose to live with the fear and my condition. It seemed to occur about once a year to start, then every six months. When I did reluctantly see a few specialists, they all suggested the same solution, a pacemaker, which I didn't want. My heart was strong. I was healthy, I reasoned. Besides, I had a business to take care of.

But over the next few years, the fear my heart issues created made everything more difficult. In particular, travel, including my trips to India and Nepal, caused me great stress.

The fear was only one more strain on my life—and on my relationship with Lila. On the surface, we had everything. We had our son, Rama, a thriving business in Pacific Spirit, a beautiful home and acres of land, and animals like Bhima and Lucifer all around us. We had a team of people who believed in what we were doing. We had our spiritual practices and our gurus who led us gently toward enlightenment.

But we also had the grief from the loss of the yogini, the stress of running a major business, the trouble of raising a teenager, and the fear that sat upon my chest, holding us back from potential trips or needed time apart.

We were growing apart, Lila and I. And soon, I would find out just how far apart we had drifted in the second dark night of my soul.

WHERE DOES THE SOUL GO?

Becoming pregnant had been a dream come true for Lila, and it was lost in an instant. Afterward, I tried to find the yogini in my meditations, but I never found her. It was because she had fully awakened in her spiritual consciousness.

You see, for most people, when they die, they spend time between lives before taking birth again. It's a continuous cycle. But each material life is really just a cover—a role you're playing, a costume you're putting on. The emotional, mental, and intellectual bodies of this physical existence cover our true soul. As Shakespeare said, "All the world's a stage, and all the men and women merely players. They have their exits and their entrances."

We are blocked, covered over by illusion (Maya), from perceiving this reality. Maya is what makes life so attractive and unattractive at the same time. To see beyond this, we must as Jesus reminds us, "Be in the world but not of the world." All of reality exists all at once and everywhere. Seeds of karma from our previous lives stay with us from material life to material life. That's why, when people die and are brought back, they'll often describe seeing their whole life flash before their eyes. They'll see their whole family appear—including members they don't recognize. This is their family across lives.

This karma tethers us to the material world and blinds us to true reality.

Wisdom, awakening, and realization burn these seeds of karma away. Once you're fully awakened, you no longer have any seeds of karma to burn away, and you leave no residue. Your aura is clean, and you are purified. There is no more heaven, and there is no more hell. You're just you—your soul—without the need for the costume, role, or covering. You no longer have the desire to take birth.

So where did the Yogini go?

She awakened from the need to take material birth. It is likely that her time as a fetus was the last seed of karma she had left to burn. Perhaps she had an abortion or lost a child in a previous life and needed to experience that from the perspective of a fetus. Regardless, she needed to work off past karma that required a physical body. Her experience complete, she was ready to reawaken into the finer realities of a pure spirit soul.

CHAPTER 10

ANOTHER DARK NIGHT

BY 2000, PACIFIC SPIRIT WAS STILL GROWING, BUT LILA and I were falling apart.

We had about thirty-five employees, and demand was still growing. It seemed as if everything we touched turned to gold, but to me, it had become very draining. The previous years had taken a toll. Through no one's fault, the loss of the yogini had wedged us apart. I was always worried when I would have my next heart episode and was fearful of leaving the country. Each time I returned from an adventure that required travel of any distance, I had thought that I dodged another bullet.

My relationship with Lila also continued to become more strained. For years, we had lived, played, traveled, and worked as one. But somewhere along the way, the happiness started to fade and stress filled the space where happiness once resided. It got to the point where we could no longer solve our problems together. I felt like I couldn't speak to Lila, and I started to mentally check myself out of the relationship. For a while, I convinced myself this was fixable, that this rough patch would pass. But as time went on, it became increasingly more difficult to argue this was a patch and not new terrain.

As things grew darker in our relationship, Lila and I started spending more time apart. But we also tried to branch out into new friendships together. It was just easier being together if there were others with us. In particular, we started spending time with our neighbors. A mile away from our farm, there were two families. On the left was Pam and Preston; to the right was Kurt and Susan.

At the time, we weren't that close to Pam and Preston. But we did become friendly with Kurt and Susan. Lila and Susan became running partners. They even ran some marathons together. Slowly, the four of us all became friends.

In one of those coincidences that are not coincidences, I recalled that we'd actually met Kurt many years before. Kurt was a contractor, and Lila had called him to give us a quote on remodeling our bathroom. He was tall like me, but barrel chested and balding. I used to joke that he looked a bit like a neanderthal, but I heard from lady friends that many would consider him attractive. At the time, Lila had refused to spend time around him. She was very respectful of our relationship and protected it.

When Kurt came over to discuss the work, Lila told me afterward, "I don't care if you hire the guy, but I don't want him around. I don't want to be near the guy."

On some level, she was aware of the direction her karma was leading her.

Perhaps I was, too. From the start, I was quite uncomfortable with this growing connection we'd formed with Kurt and Susan. I once had a vision that Lila or I was going to have an affair with Kurt or Susan. When I told Lila, she said that if anyone was going to have an affair, it was me. She'd always been afraid

I was going to cheat during our relationship. I couldn't imagine myself with Susan, but I left it at that.

I had no idea how right my vision was.

Despite my discomfort, I tried to embrace our newfound friends. I invited Kurt and Susan to take one of my *Bhagavad-gita* classes. We'd sit in their hot tub and talk through passages. I began to go with Lila and Susan when they'd run around a track. I'd ride my bike. Sometimes, Kurt would come along with Susan. Then, one day, Kurt showed up without Susan. He made some half excuse for her absence, but it was clear from the first moment this wasn't a one-time thing. Susan wasn't sick. Susan wasn't coming anymore.

"This is a bad idea," I said to Lila, but she insisted it was fine.

"Kurt's my friend, too," she said.

The woman who had once refused to even meet Kurt for fear of harming our relationship set off on a run alone with him, her husband watching on.

I couldn't believe my eyes.

A NEW LAWSUIT

The situation with Kurt was serious, but I didn't have much time to focus on it. On top of the heart issues, the emergency room visits, and marital tension, Pacific Spirit was also facing a lawsuit for one of our intellectual properties.

We owned the US trademark for "Whole Life," under the category of catalog sales and gift items. There was another company called Whole Life Expo that held the trademark for that phrase for temporary events, such as conferences, expos, and shows. We had both been in business for the same amount of time, and there was never an issue between us until the internet came on the scene. Whole Life Expo wanted to place their expo online and invite everyone with a product to be a part of their website. But this was an infringement to our trademark.

We sent them a cease and desist letter and their slimy attorney asked us to wait a few weeks so that they could discuss it. In the meantime, he filed a suit against us in California, asking a judge to stop us. Next thing I knew, I was being ordered by a federal judge to show up in her courtroom in San Francisco.

Whole Life Expo had insurance and wanted to fight us for our trademark. We had insurance, too, but our insurance company, slime that they were, said that since we were the ones suing, they were not going to cover our damages.

So we sued our insurance company, as well. Eventually, we won the trademark suit, but it took three years to see a penny from the insurance company. By that time, the full award went to our attorney to cover this drawn out battle. In the end, it cost us $175,000 to keep what Pacific Spirit already owned.

Another great day in court for the Kenzers.

THE LAST TRIP TOGETHER

With everything going on, I was beginning to lose a sense of who I was. Struggling through another court case, my instinct was to turn to Lila for mutual support, but the distance between us only continued to grow. We no longer fit into the Mark-and-Lila frame. Lila and I were no longer one. We had always joked about sharing the same brain, but now we were becoming emotionally and mentally removed from each other.

The scalpel of our buried karma had cut its way through our invisible past, and we didn't know how to bring it back together. We had never before had serious differences that we couldn't solve on our own, but now even external issues couldn't bring us together.

Maybe if Lila and I got away together, I thought, we could reconnect and remember how much we loved each other. One of our friends and business associates, Abdel, was going on a buying trip to China and had invited us to join him. I was so afraid of traveling, but I really felt we needed the time away.

At first, Lila was resistant.

"Mark, why don't you just go by yourself?" she suggested. "You know I don't like to fly."

It was true. For all my fear of traveling because of my heart condition, Lila also had trouble with planes. In the past, she had repeatedly dreamed about airplane crashes. Her dreams, like mine, were deeply prophetic. Very often, she would wake and tell me her dream, only for us to find out later that day that the event actually took place while we were asleep. We made quite a pair of overseas travelers.

"You know I can't go alone," I pleaded with her. "Please go with me."

After much convincing, Lila agreed to accompany me on the trip. I had gotten what I wanted, but for days I couldn't sleep. I really didn't want to go, but I also couldn't stay. Something had to change, and this was the best excuse for change that I could come up with.

I had a foreboding sense that something terrible was about to happen—not so different from my feeling before flying to Toronto. Thanks to my insomnia, I started having dreamlike hallucinations in which I was in the underworld with hideous creatures and dark forces surrounding me. I eventually needed sleep medication just to get some rest.

The feeling of dread continued to escalate. A few days before our departure, during my morning meditation, I prayed for help, "God, if something's going to happen to me, please have it happen here and not on the plane or in some other country."

He's going to die.

My fear of death was at its peak.

That evening, we went to a Krishna temple in Portland for the Sunday feast. My heart once again began to race.

"Lila, you need to take me to the hospital," I said. I was flat-lined again in the ER that night.

The next day, I called Abdel and told him I couldn't go to China. My nerves had become so frayed, I couldn't even drive on the freeway. I was so afraid something would happen to me. But Abdel talked me through it—these episodes were happening at most twice a year at this point. Having just had one, there was a good chance I wouldn't have another during this trip.

Abdel convinced me. The next morning, Lila and I flew to Los Angeles—a thankfully uneventful flight—where we boarded our international flight to Hong Kong to meet Abdel. As we waited at the gate to board, I suddenly froze in fear.

"Lila, I'm scared, tell me what to do," I said. For a moment, I even tried blaming it on her. "You made me go," I blurted out, immediately knowing that was a mistake. I didn't even feel in control of myself at that point.

I thought again of the time I was in this same airport, over-whelmed with fear before my flight to meet the devil in Toronto. Only then, I'd had Sandy's spiritual support to guide me through. I didn't have that same support from Lila now.

A stewardess from the flight came out one more time to get us. "That was the last call," she said. "We are going to close the door. You need to board now."

We both got up automatically and followed. Airborne, our shared panic only intensified.

"Lila, I'm afraid," I said. "I'm sorry that I got on this flight."

But Lila was just as scared. "Don't tell me that," she replied. "I'm sorry. I don't know what to do."

Neither of us could deliver the comfort the other needed.

I don't know how, but I did survive that flight and, eventually, the plane landed in Hong Kong. My heart was still pounding, my body was shaking, my nerves were totally shot. I was thankful when we were on the ground at last, but my mind immediately turned to my next worries—there were modern hospitals in Hong Kong, but what about mainland China? There was no end to my worry and stress.

Some vacation.

For the following week, we shopped in Hong Kong with Abdel. My heart would not stop pounding. It was running overtime, and I could feel that my blood pressure was greatly elevated.

"Lila, I can't continue like this, I want to go home," I said.

I tried waiting a few more days and then gave up and changed our reservation to fly home early. Lila, at this point, no longer wanted to have anything to do with me. So much for sharing our lives together. I could feel that things were coming to an abrupt end. I worried it was going to be my end, as well.

The day of our flight home, I swam at the hotel pool until exhausted in an effort to tire myself out so I could sleep on the plane, something I always struggled with. Then, we headed to the airport for our overnight flight.

I didn't dare say a word to Lila. I knew that I had to get on this flight and wanted to get myself home. Shortly after the plane took off, I fell asleep. The next thing I heard was the announcement that we had begun our descent into LAX.

"Wow, that is great," I said. I had never slept so well. All I could recall was taking off. I had absolutely no recollection of the thirteen-hour fight.

Our arrival back in America—combined with the prospect of no further flights—eased things between Lila and I. We decided that we didn't want to go back home yet.

"How about we get a hotel and go someplace sunny tomorrow, like Sedona?" I suggested.

So, we checked into a hotel in Los Angeles, and we both went back to sleep. Suddenly, Lila bolted up in bed and grabbed my arm.

"Mark, wake up," she said, shaking me awake. "I just had a very strange vision. I know what is happening and why you were so afraid."

I was now sitting up next to her. "Tell me what you saw."

"I dreamt that the airplane that we boarded had crashed, and I could see the wreckage all over the runway," she said distressed. "People were screaming and there were fires all over. The black smoke was thick, and we were floating over the carnage. You were shaking me to wake up, but I couldn't accept what had happened. You kept saying, 'Lila, you have to wake up, it's time for us to move on. We have died in this plane crash. You have to wake up. We need to move on.'"

I had no reason to doubt what she was saying. I had absolutely no memory of what happened after take off.

"But Lila, we were just in Hong Kong with Abdel, don't you remember?" I said. "And we boarded a plane for Los Angeles, and now we are here."

"No, Mark," Lila said. "You just think that. The plane crashed shortly after take off. And that's why you think that you were asleep, but you've been trying to wake me up so that we could move on. We're dead. And we're just thinking that we are still alive. We are actually dead and have to wake up."

I didn't know what to make of it. Everything that she was saying made sense. Quantum physics tells us these things are actually possible—that the plane did crash, but in another dimension. It occured in another universe outside of the one we were conscious in. Vasistha's Yoga scripture of India, too, confirms the possibility of this. It describes stories of living in different realities at the same time.

Perhaps Lila, recognizing her own life was crashing down around her, sought out a memory of this other reality.

I wasn't sure if I wanted to accept this as true. But it didn't really matter. At that moment, we were only conscious of being in a hotel in Los Angeles. At that moment, I had no choice but to live in the reality where I felt present.

The next day, we took a flight to Phoenix and spent a few days in Sedona before heading back to our "reality," such as it was.

But it was a reality we were reluctant to meet, one filled with more death and parting.

GOODBYE TO GOOD FRIENDS

In this period, I was increasingly isolated. Not only was Lila drifting away, Rama was too. Throughout his childhood, Rama and I had always been close. As he reached late adolescence, though, he followed his natural inclinations to become more independent and rebellious.

This would have been no more than a normal period of conflict between parents and son, except Lila and I were no longer on the same team. Instead, she took Rama's side. Rama, sensing increasing tension between us, used it as an opportunity.

In previous years, I might have turned to my animal companions for support with my troubles, but we were entering an era in which we had to walk the long road to goodbye. As is the case with all aging dogs, Bhima was showing his age. He started taking longer to get up when he'd been lying down, walking more slowly, and his snout had turned gray.

One day, I realized I hadn't seen Bhima in a while and went

outside to check on him. I found him lying on the hot coals of our burn pile. I could see the red glow coming from the wood embers. My first thought was that he must have laid himself there to die.

I called his name and got no response. I called out again, nothing. Finally, the third time, he woke up. He stood up and shook off the embers as he made his way over to me. I'd never seen anything like this. I could feel the heat from the coals, but Bhima seemed to be impervious, his fur insulating him just like it did when he would sleep in the snow in winter.

But this miraculous respite from death was temporary. One afternoon shortly thereafter, I could see in Bhima's eyes that he was going to leave his body that evening. We all said our goodbyes, and I spent the evening outside with him. To this day, I still feel bad that I went inside to sleep. When I woke up, I went to look for Bhima, but I knew he was already gone. He was lying on the front lawn, a place he rarely visited.

I loaded his hard body into the pickup truck. Our other dog, Jeeva, jumped in. We drove out to a nice spot in our field and began to dig a large hole. When the hole was large enough, we dragged Bhima off the truck and placed him in it.

Just as we were about to cover his body with earth, Jeeva did something that deeply touched our hearts—she leaped from the truck and stood over Bhima's body to protect him. Tears poured from her nose and eyes. She had lost her friend and didn't know what to do.

Lila and I looked on, crying. We knew it was time for Bhima to move on, but we felt the same as Jeeva.

After losing Bhima, my relationship with Lila suffered even further strain. Another connection between us had been severed. At least I still had Lucifer.

Though Lila and I saw each other every day, we rode less

frequently together. That meant that, if I wanted to ride, I'd have to go on my own. Being herd animals, horses usually prefer to be near other horses and are much calmer when they are. We shared this desire—to always be near our herd. But, given the new circumstances, both Lucifer and I were forced to ride alone.

One day I decided to push our boundaries and we rode off to a farm area we had never visited before to explore the bank of a creek. The next thing I knew, we were sliding down the bank. Lucifer was up to his shoulders in mud and gravel. He was in so deep he struggled to get himself out. Gently, I removed his saddle, and after much effort and my pulling on the reins, we broke Lucifer free.

As we walked back up the embankment, I could see the cuts on both of our legs. I put the saddle back on Lucifer but didn't plan to ride him—he had been through enough.

"We can walk back together," I told him, but Lucifer wouldn't have it. He just stood there, waiting. I pulled gently on his lead, and he braced himself, looking at me with his large, gentle, brown eyes. He wanted to finish the job and take me back. I tried again to encourage him to walk on, but he refused. I got back up, and we rode home together. We were bonding in a way we never had before.

On another excursion, Lucifer and I were coming down a very steep forested mountain. Because it was wet and muddy, I dismounted and led Lucifer down on foot. But soon, I started to slide down the hill, with Lucifer bearing down on me like a locomotive, his breath pumping and warm vapors from his nostrils hitting my face. We slid down the incline face to face, and finally came to a stop at the bottom. Relieved and safe at last, we rode back home. After that, we had become even more of a team.

Yet, despite all his strength, bravery, and devotion, Lucifer was also leaving me. A few days after our ride, Lucifer did not look well. When the vet came out, I learned he had contracted pigeon fever. While the illness often manifests on the outside of a horse's chest, Lucifer's fever was inside his body, and it was eating away at his life energy. After running bloodwork, the vet told me Lucifer's numbers were very high and there wasn't much we could do except give him medicine and hope he pulled through.

Twice a day, I shot a large syringe of overpriced medicine down Lucifer's throat, and he tolerated it with grace. But his eyes said that he was scared, or perhaps he was just reflecting my fears.

Very soon, Lucifer's weight started dropping and all I could do was love him, brush him, and hope to God that he would pull through.

A month went by, and the medicine was almost gone. It seemed to have done its work. Lucifer was looking good, bright-eyed and sturdy, but still weak. I called the vet back out for blood work. He, too, was impressed by his recovery, but the numbers on his bloodwork told a different story. He told me he would likely die very soon.

I got off the phone and tried to hold back the tears. I had just given Lucifer another dose of the medicine, but this time he spit it back out. He already knew the truth.

He's going to die.

So this was how my mother had felt when the doctor had spoken those words.

"I'm afraid that you're not going to make it," I told Lucifer, crying. "And I don't know what else to do for you. It's your body. And if you no longer want the medicine, I won't force you to take it. Just let me know what I can do for you."

For the next few days, I could hardly face going out to see

Lucifer, I could see how frail he was becoming. I started giving him lots of carrots, knowing that at one time in my life, carrot juice had helped heal me of a number of health issues. Lucifer loved them, and in response, he gave me one last gift. Before I knew it, his weight began to increase. He was still much weaker than he had been before he was sick, but he eventually became strong enough that he could ride again.

We just walked around for about ten minutes and that was enough. I could tell he was happy to have me on his back. We continued this routine as he grew stronger and stronger. Sometimes, I invented chores he could help me with. It gave us an excuse to ride around together.

Riding Lucifer after he'd been ill not only helped him regain his strength, but it tied our spirits together forever. I used to hear how deeply someone could connect with a horse—I had connections with my dogs growing up, and I definitely had it with Bhima. And now, Lucifer and I had that connection, too.

Then one morning, I went out to see Lucifer and found him lying down at the bottom of the lowest pasture. I was keeping him in one of the upper pastures, so I knew that something must have happened for him to go through the electric fence to get to this spot. But there was no break anywhere in the fence.

I called his name, but like Bhima on the hot coal, he just laid there. Mentally, I prepared myself for the worst.

What I saw made my stomach drop. Lucifer's skin was rubbed all the way down to the muscle on the sides of his head, on his flanks and shoulders. It was as if someone had torched him with fire. The grass all around him was completely worn, blackened from being rubbed. How had he ended up down here? It didn't make sense.

He raised his head to look at me. He looked exhausted and struggled to get up. I called Lila, and she and I walked him up to the stall where he could get some water. He was dehydrated and drank gallon after gallon, but wouldn't accept any carrots.

When the vet arrived, she suggested he had colic, which can cause such pain that a horse thrashes and rolls around vigorously. As they do this, they twist their digestive tract and, shortly after, they die.

The vet said that there was nothing else we could do. The only large animal hospital was three hours away and the surgery to untwist the tract was so high risk, Lucifer likely wouldn't survive.

There would be no miraculous recovery this time.

The vet suggested putting him down, but for me, this was out of the question. Lucifer had been through a lot in his life. I knew he would want to die a proud death on his own, regardless of the pain. She told me this could be hard to watch and told me to call her if I changed my mind.

Lucifer and I spent a number of hours together on that final day. I talked to him, brushed him, and let him know how much I appreciated him for all of our years together. We walked together, stood and talked. I watched as he came to terms with his inevitable death.

His bravery impressed me. I thought back to my own crippling fear getting on the plane to Hong Kong and my terror traveling out of reach of a modern doctor. How much I still had to learn about detachment from material life. Lucifer was still teaching me on his final day, as all great wise souls do.

I wanted to be there when he died, but the vet was right—this was extremely difficult to witness. As the evening descended, Lucifer started to paw and thrash. The other horses kept their distance as they watched their majestic friend lose the ability to stand. Each time he fell, Lucifer would struggle to get back up. I asked him to please stay down, but this wasn't his nature. He always rose to the occasion.

It was almost midnight. Lucifer continued to struggle, as if he had wanted to make it just one more day. Perhaps the morning would bring new light into his now-darkened life. I moved away from him as he struggled one last time to get up. Then, I heard him fall for the last time. It was a fall unlike the others.

Lucifer was gone. His black body with his four white socks was all that remained. I covered him with a deep purple warmer that I had made for him—*Lucifer, the vision of light* was engraved in bright yellow thread. My boy had moved on to greener pastures.

And I was more alone than ever.

THINGS FALL APART

I had lost my best animal companions, and now, finally, I was about to lose my marriage.

After years of growing distant, the end announced itself in a prophetic act. Jesús, our warehouse manager at Pacific Spirit, and I were moving some heavy lumber together when the load fell on my ring finger. My wedding ring actually shielded it from being completely smashed, but before I knew it, the finger started to swell. It was now larger than my middle finger.

"Jesús, I need you to cut my ring off," I winced in pain. My whole hand was starting to throb.

Jesús grabbed a wire cutter and drove it under the ring, slowly making a snip. The ring flew about fifty feet across the barn. After finding it, we decided to break for lunch.

"Well, this isn't a good omen," I said to Lila as I walked into the kitchen where she was cooking. I showed her my slashed wedding ring that now looked like the letter *C*.

"What do you mean by that? What happened?" she asked, sounding irritated. I told her what happened. She didn't appreciate me taking it as an omen, but how could I not? The signs were all there. Our difficulties had so increased, I was currently sleeping in another room at night.

A few days later, I went out to run an errand. Usually, when I drove somewhere by myself, I would take the truck and leave the car for Lila, but that day for whatever reason, I took the car. As I pulled back into the garage, I happened to glance back and noticed a jacket lying in the backseat. I must have left it the last time Lila and I drove together, I thought. As I reached back to pick it up, however, my heart sank.

This wasn't my jacket.

I identified the true owner immediately—Kurt, our neighbor. I recognized in this feeling a familiar suspicion that had been growing over the past few weeks.

I cautiously made my way into the house, reviewing my words with each step. My vision of my own home had started to change, and suddenly, I felt extremely unwelcome. Lila loomed in the living room. I had never seen her like this, as some traitor I had to interrogate, but it was her, my wife, the person that I had given my life to.

"What is Kurt's jacket doing in our car?" I asked.

"What do you mean? He probably left it there."

She began to spin a story that would explain things, but it didn't matter. She said one thing, but my gut was telling me another.

"Don't make something more out of this than it is," she said, getting defensive. "You always think you know, but you don't. Nothing is going on between us."

I did know, but I wanted to believe the only person I had ever been able to trust completely. I tried to accept her explanation, but after finding the jacket, I became more aware of Lila's whereabouts during the day. With eyes open, it wasn't difficult to see that she would disappear for an hour or two each day without telling me where she was going. Or if she did tell me and I offered to go with her, she always declined, insisting she needed some "alone time."

One afternoon, Kurt showed up at our house just as we were sitting down for lunch.

"Why is Kurt here?" I asked as he was making his way up the driveway. "It's funny how he started coming around more. Why doesn't he spend more time with his own family?"

Lila just tried to brush it off.

"He's our friend," she said. "He always comes around if he knows there's food."

"Lila, he has a wife, and she is your friend," I replied. "Does she know that he comes here?" She just looked away.

As we sat down to lunch this particular afternoon, I couldn't look Kurt in the eye. Every time I looked at him, I reflexively looked away. It was like my body was confirming the truth. After Kurt left, I mustered the courage to confront Lila.

"You and Kurt are having an affair," I said to her point blank. "Why don't you just admit it?"

"We're not having an affair," Lila said. "You are stressed. Just because things are not working between us doesn't mean that Kurt and I are having an affair."

"Swear to Krishna that you're not having an affair," I said. This was something that Rama and his friends used to say when the situation demanded the truth—"swear to God." Lila and I had adapted this into our lives as an opportunity to come clean should the occasion arise for any of us.

It was easy. Yay or nay. Either you swear or you aren't willing to admit the truth. We could end this in a moment with no questions asked.

"Swear to Krishna?" I asked again as I watched Lila struggle.

There was no need to struggle with the truth—unless the truth was something she couldn't bear to admit.

"What do you think, that I'm Rama?" she responded, flustered and buying time. "I can't believe you're asking me this."

I knew it was over. Nonetheless, I continued asking why she wouldn't answer.

"Ok, I swear to Krishna," she said.

"Swear what?" I prodded.

"That I'm not having an affair."

That was not what I expected. Now what was I to do? I knew what I was feeling wasn't just coming from me. Our relationship was in trouble. I also knew that I wanted out of the relationship very badly. I was hurting and didn't know where to turn. I felt responsible for all the employees. I felt responsible for paying off the mortgages we had. I felt responsible for doing the right thing for Rama. And I felt responsible to myself.

My heart was breaking again, but this time, it went much deeper than racing and pounding in arrhythmic disorder. My heart was crying from the inside, and there was no one to wipe my tears. I felt alienated and alone.

With no allies, I turned to God. My whole adult life, I'd meditated and read spiritual books. This is how I learned to change my life and where I got my answers. It was also how I adjusted to all the evil and the wrongs that I saw being perpetrated in the world. Meditation was my path, and God and my guru guided me. So I tried to immerse myself on a deeper level into my practice.

One day I was reading a story in the *Srimad Bhagavatam*, a vast scriptural work of 18,000 verses composed by Veda-vyasa, and I ran across this verse:

"Once a group of large Hawks who were unable to find any prey attacked another weaker Hawk who was holding some meat at that time. Being in danger of his life, the Hawk gave up his meat and experienced actual happiness" (Canto 11.9.2).

That was it, my answer: I just had to drop the meat. It became my mantra. Anytime I was in trouble, I tried to follow those instructions.

"Drop the meat. Just drop the meat, Mark," I'd say to myself.

Unfortunately, I didn't know how. Like the smaller bird, I was running in fear, but I couldn't quite let go of my "meat"— the money, sex, love, pride, success, and everything else that the ego had led me to believe was me. Lucifer had known how to drop the meat and face separation with bravery, but not I.

My heart wanted to follow this example and get out. It just didn't know how to do it. But, I convinced myself, I was going to fix that, just like I was going to fix my relationship with Lila.

I remained paralyzed in indecision, struggling to accept the end of what had already ended.

I found myself pacing around our house. Back and forth, like a panther I strode. I must have been doing this for some time when it hit me. I am like an animal trapped in a cage. I'm a caged animal, and I see no way out.

I sat to meditate. As I meditated, I could see Lila and Kurt having sex. It made me so sick. I tried to put the thought out of my mind, but it kept flashing in my consciousness, making me feel all the worse.

Now, I knew that I not only wanted out, but I had to be the one to make the move. Lila was as blocked as I was. As with our flight to Hong Kong, we were both frozen in fear.

"I'm sorry," she had said then. "I don't know what to do."

Both of us paralyzed, we had been unable to do anything but board the plane and let it take us to our fate—a fate in which we died in some dimension of existence. We were on such a flight now, and neither of us could change its direction nor speed it up. We would reach the end when the end arrived.

At this point, we had crossed the ocean of separation, but still we taxied in the air, unable to reach our final destination—the moment of rupture. Around and around we went, tortured by the delay, powerless to speed it up.

One evening, I walked into the house and saw the light blink on the phone—a sign someone had left a voicemail. The phone line was part of the same phone system that we had in our other buildings. I noticed that the call was on our personal home line, and the phone system had already sent it to voicemail.

I picked up the receiver. There was talking, and what I heard dropped on my heart like hot solder. It was Lila. Apparently, she was calling to check her messages and was reviewing messages that she and Kurt had left each other. Stealthily, she had set up a secret voice mailbox so they could leave love messages to each other.

My heart seized up. I almost died. Dying would have been easier than going through this!

After hearing a handful of the messages, I hung up and cried. I wanted to throw up, but instead, I lay on the floor, holding my guts.

A few days later, Lila came by the house to talk about "working things out." She had moved to a townhouse a few miles away by then, saying she needed her space. We were still taxiing through the air, deluding each other that this was temporary or fixable.

For a time, I sat there with my broken heart, listening to my wife deliver one line after another. Finally, I could take no more.

"Lila, I know that you have been seeing Kurt," I said.

"Stop it, Mark. You don't know what you're talking about," Lila shook her head.

I just looked at her and cried.

"Lila, I heard the messages that you left for each other. "

"How did you do that?" She was still looking for a way out. "What did you hear?"

I told her what I had heard and she started crying, ashamed. She ran out the door into the night.

That was my hardest night. This was one of the nights that I hoped to die in my sleep.

A few days after this, I left for Los Angeles to do some buying at Abdel's. He and I had become close over the years. He and his wife, Laila, always invited me to stay in their home. One morning, Abdel and I were sitting at breakfast and making small talk.

"Mark is something wrong?" he asked.

I couldn't hold it in any longer. Tears are welling up within my eyes. My voice started to crack.

"Abdel, Lila is having an affair, and she's not willing to admit it."

Abdel put his hand on mine and told me how he had been through the same thing and offered his help in any way.

Once in Portland, I had planned to take the light rail home from the airport, but Lila offered to pick me up. The whole ride home, I could tell she was trying to be herself, but the tension between us kept us apart.

"Can we talk?" Lila asked once we'd reached the house.

"Sure. Let's go out to the back deck and get some fresh air." I sensed I was going to need it.

Lila fidgeted around a little. I knew what was coming, but this would still be one of the hardest moments of my entire life.

Finally—finally—Lila landed the plane.

"Mark, I'm having an affair with Kurt," Lila said.

My whole being just sank. My legs went weak. A small voice inside me said, "Brace yourself, there's more. Ask her what else she has to say."

I hated this inner voice of reason. Why couldn't I let go of that part of me that identified what was happening in the moment? Why did I still struggle after all these years of spiritual practice to detach myself from the present I was experiencing? Why was the pain still so real?

"There's more, isn't there?" I closed my eyes. Here it came.

"Yes, Mark," Lila said softly. "I'm pregnant."

As soon as these two words left her lips, I could see all of my energy as a force of inner light traveling collectively down my body out the bottom of my spine. I dropped to my knees and cried.

"No, no, no."

There was no way I could continue in this relationship with Lila. I just rolled onto my side and sobbed, wondering how I could have continued partially participating in this relationship for so long.

ONE LAST DELUSION

At least it was over. At least we had finally crashed the plane and could try to leave the wreckage behind. Or so I thought.

Days later, Lila asked me to go into therapy with her. I agreed but doubted that it was going to help much. I needed time away. But Lila said that she didn't have time. When the therapist asked why I didn't think it was going to work, I told him it was because Lila was still seeing Kurt. It took the therapist a few minutes to convince Lila that this arrangement wasn't going to work if she wanted to salvage our relationship. Finally, Lila agreed to stop.

We saw the therapist for a few weeks. On the morning of one of our sessions, I went to the gym before the appointment. It was the same gym Lila and I had joined along with Kurt and Susan a few years prior.

After my workout, I stopped on my way out to drop off my locker key. The young man working at the desk, who I would frequently chat with, asked me, "Who's Kurt?" It was obvious by his head tilted like a puppy dog that something wasn't making sense to him. Suddenly, the light went on. "Oh, Kurt was here with Lila?"

"Yes, they come together all the time," the man said. "He acts as if she's his wife."

Lila was still seeing Kurt.

I thanked him and headed to our appointment, hating the therapist almost as much as I hated Lila. This wasn't going to work. Why couldn't he see that? I saw it. The session started as usual, with Lila talking first.

"Blah, blah, blah, blah, blah," was all I heard.

Then, it was my turn.

"Lila is still seeing Kurt," I blurted out.

Lila tried to explain to the therapist this was all because I didn't trust her. Finally, he stopped her and asked what was going on. I told him what the man at the gym had said.

Lila started to look around. I knew her instinct to run instead of face the truth from her behavior after I heard her phone messages. But this time, she would have to go by me and the therapist if she was going to make it out the door. She started getting smaller, just like in the cartoons when the character has been caught lying. All eyes were on her. She lifted her hands to block her face.

I started to get up and leave, "I'm outta here."

"Please wait, give her a chance," the therapist said. "I want to hear what Lila has to say." It was a request I was willing to grant. I wanted him to see that I had been right, but I also wanted to prove to myself that my intuition had been correct all along. Lila had almost convinced me that my sensitivities—which had so often seen the future and beyond this reality—were somehow lying to me. Now, I could prove that I had been right, and I had been wasting my time, money, and most importantly, my life.

Lila just looked at him with the eyes of a drowning woman. What was our therapist going to say now? I waited to hear what pearls of wisdom were about to spew from his mouth.

But what he said actually moved me, "All you have is the truth."

Not even Lila could argue her way out of that one. She admitted that she had been seeing Kurt.

I got up and left. The therapist tried to stop me and suggested that we meet for a closing session. Right. He might have needed closure, but I sure didn't. Not now, not anymore. Lila had tried to get that broken plane airborne again, but I knew for certain it was no more than scrap.

KARMA

We are all spiritual living energy that has existed from the beginning of time. We keep taking birth in a body during which we are covered over by our mental makeup, our parents, and our society—and we are also influenced by our karma.

This karma exists on every plane of our existence, and it's not all bad. It's an accumulation of energy that must be burned off or else manifest in the material world. Little seeds will grow into mature fruit, if not destroyed with wisdom or positive actions. Once germinated with desire, they will grow and multiply.

For instance, as a child, my goal was to have a million dollars. This desire was clearly introduced because of my karma. As soon as Pacific Spirit made a million dollars, I lost interest in the business. Lila couldn't believe it, but it no longer had any meaning to me beyond the help it offered others. I had to see that karma manifested in material life. Once it did, I burned it off and moved on.

Karma was clearly in play throughout this period in my life. Lila initially tried to avoid Kurt because she sensed that her karma would manifest in this affair. Likewise, her lifelong fear of plane crashes connected back to her karma from a past life. That plane crashed in some reality because of karma that Lila carried with her into this life.

Though we might try to avoid karma, it's impossible for the simple reason that these events have already happened.

Though we experience time linearly, that isn't the nature of existence. Time is really consciousness. So long as we identify with our body and the ego thinks that s/he is the doer, we will be affected by that karma. It is only once the spirit soul identifies with his or her actual position as part of God that karma no longer affects him/her.

This enlightened perspective requires immense spiritual growth. We can see this in how Jesus addresses Peter before his arrest. He tells Peter that the disciple will betray the master three times that night. Peter can't believe it. Despite his supreme spiritual advancement, his ego still tied him to the material world. He couldn't see, as Jesus could, that this had happened. It already was.

This is what enabled me to know that Lila was going to have an affair. It was part of our shared karma, and it had already happened. Of course, when it manifested in the material world, it still hurt, just the same. But dealing with it—and going through the divorce—could help burn that karma off, and eventually, allow me to move on and progress into my third awakening.

∾

CHAPTER 11

MORE GOODBYES

AFTER THE DIVORCE, I WAS LIVING IN OUR HOME—THE one that we had built together—on my own while Lila stayed in her rented condo.

I slept in the downstairs of the farmhouse, unable to venture up the stairs to where we had made love and shared so much intimacy for almost fifteen years. As I worked to make sense of things, I found myself telling anyone and everyone who would listen "my story." Somehow, with each telling, it got a little easier to accept.

The only person I did not burden with my tale was my friend, Dan Potter. Dan and his wife, Jan, lived about a mile down the road. They'd moved to Oregon years ago from New Hampshire, and we became friends in a rather roundabout way, linked by our shared spirituality.

When Dan and Jan had first arrived in Oregon, they had bought sandwiches at a health food store. The sandwiches were made by Higher Taste, a vegetarian food company owned by my old friends Hans and Rhonda—the ones I had visited in upstate New York when I met Staz many years ago. Hans and Rhonda had moved to Oregon years earlier.

Knowing that all Hare Krishnas are vegetarian, Dan and Jan called the phone number on the sandwich label and asked Hans and Rhonda if they knew any Hare Krishnas in the area they could connect with. Back then, this was often how vegetarians found restaurants and grocery stores that would cater to their diets. Hans and Rhonda had only one way to point them—to me and Lila.

Dan and Jan were not Hare Krishnas themselves, but they were interested in Hare Krishna philosophy and spiritual wisdom from any tradition that would lead them to the truth. Unsurprisingly, we became fast friends.

But now, Dan was battling lymphoma and slowly, he was dying. He told me that he wanted to work out as much karma as possible to liberate his consciousness with transcendental knowledge so that he could leave his body and go back to the spiritual world.

I visited him daily. He was slowly losing his eyesight, so I would read to him every afternoon from the *Srimad Bhagavatam* until he was too tired to listen. With each day the cancer progressed, I noticed his realizations would deepen and increase, and he became more detached from the material world.

One afternoon, Dan shared with me a story about his first experience with Krishna, also known as Lord Vishnu. At the time, Dan was a freshman in high school. A friend had received a book from a Hare Krishna devotee while in the city. The book contained an image of Lord Vishnu on the cover—a copy of the *Bhagavad-gita*. Intrigued, Dan headed to the city to meet the Hare Krishnas himself.

He'd never told anyone this before, but just before he got into town, Dan had a heatstroke and died. He told me how, as soon as he fell on the sidewalk, he saw a bright light that led to a tunnel. He was immediately drawn into it and traveled through it for what seemed like miles. Emerging out of the tunnel, he saw several relatives, all from the past. Some he recognized, others he did not, but they all wanted him to go with them.

Then, Dan looked past his relatives and there, to the left, he saw Jesus. Jesus extended his arm to direct Dan further beyond where he stood. Dan followed his direction and saw the form of Lord Vishnu. Jesus was leading Dan home to God.

Suddenly, Dan was forcibly pulled back through the tunnel. He opened his eyes and found himself lying in a hospital bed.

"I always attributed this happening to the fact that I had seen and touched the *Bhagavad-gita*," Dan told me. "It was enough to wake me up and take me further than my Christian upbringing had."

Being in Dan's presence everyday gave me an opportunity to see the changes that everyone who was looking death in the face must come to terms with. And each day, I could see in his eyes that he had become more ready to make his journey into the arms of Bhaktivedanta Swami Prabhupada, the translator of the holy books that we were reading together—or even Lord Vishnu himself. Dan said Prabhupada had visited him in the hospital and assured him that everything was going to be all right.

The night that Dan was to leave his body, many of his friends gathered for one last Kirtan—and to say goodbye. Dan sat in his chair, his consciousness drifting from this world into the next. Though experiencing the pain of dying from cancer, Dan was extremely transcendentally happy. Everyone with him could feel this new energy that he was sharing.

Dan had enlivened all of his friends with the power of *Bhakti*, one's pure love for the Divine. As Dan would say, this is all that he had and all that he could take with him.

Early the next morning, Jan called me. "Dan left his body a few hours ago," she said.

I immediately sat to meditate to see if I could be with Dan. Soon, I felt his presence.

"Dan, where are you?" I asked.

"I don't know," he responded. "I'm waiting." I could sense that there were some other souls present with him.

"Are you alone?" I asked.

"No, Prabhupada's disciples are with me," Dan said. "They say that I have to wait here. That Prabhupada is coming and that he will take me."

There wasn't much left for me to say. I only hoped to be so fortunate. I called Jan and told her what Dan had said. She told me when their son, Christopher, had woken up that morning having dreamt of Prabhupada purifying his dad with fire.

My friend was gone from this life, but I knew he was in the best place he could be.

THE CHEATERS AND THE CHEATED

I wish I could have integrated the wisdom Dan taught me through his example, but the troubles in my life continued to grow.

I soon found myself being cheated again. This time, not by Lila, but by a once-trusted colleague named Arpo.

Bhaktivedanta Swami summed up material creation as primarily consisting of the cheaters and the cheated—or those who were willing to say and do anything and take advantage of others, and those who were always being taken advantage of.

I had encountered many cheaters in my life, and Arpo proved to be yet another.

When I first met Arpo, he was working as a manager at one

of Portland's color separation companies. This was before the digital age, and we relied heavily on color separations for our catalogs. Arpo was well-versed in his profession and an asset to our company.

One day, Arpo approached me and asked if I was willing to help him open up his own state-of-the-art facility. I had an interest in going digital, and he promised that we could do it together—he just wanted my assurance that I would become his customer if he invested in the equipment. I agreed, and soon, we were doing all of our catalog work at Arpo's new business, Catalog Creatives. Together, we helped take the first steps in the digital age, as far as catalog printing was concerned.

One day, our office manager, Lila's sister, Lorrell, was reviewing Arpo's billings with Pacific Spirit. We'd been doing business now for a number of years, and the stack of invoices from Arpo's company was over a foot tall. Lorrell had a very keen sense of overbilling deception from her previous work in accounting, and she had begun to notice that Arpo often acted uneasy and was always insisting that we owed him money. She soon discovered what she suspected: Arpo had been padding his bills to us for years—to the extent that we had overpaid him by $80,000.

The next afternoon, we sat down with Arpo in his attorney's office, where Lorrell presented her findings. There was no disproving them—numbers don't lie.

I suggested to Arpo that we assume it was an honest mistake, and that he could pay us $50,000 over time to settle the matter.

Arpo's attorney turned to him and said, "Well, what do you say, Arpo? It looks right to me."

Arpo asked for a few weeks to review.

"I'm an honest man," he said. "If I find that what you presented is correct, then I will pay you the money."

A few weeks turned into a few years.

Arpo said he had to go back to Holland to be with his dying father. When we never heard from him, we filed a lawsuit. In return, Arpo filed his own suit against me, the company, and one of our freelance artists, Naomi Sakanoue, who had designed most of our catalogs.

The suit was for copyright infringement. Arpo was claiming that we owed him $8 million and that he owned the rights to every photo in every catalog we had printed.

Arpo understood our arrangement from the get-go. Once we went digital, Naomi sketched out the positioning of the products and someone at Arpo's office would shoot it. It was work for hire, and the copyright belonged to us. I had made that clear to Arpo, and he had agreed. But there was one problem—we didn't have any of this in writing. Now, not only was he trying to avoid paying what he owed us, he had come up with a way to get rich off us in the process.

Arpo had hired two top-notch lawyers to defend him, and even though I thought it was clear we were in the right, the federal judge ruled against us in our pretrial hearing.

So we asked for a jury. Our attorney warned us: if we lose this case, there would be no settlement. We would have to give up everything. We didn't have $8 million. A loss would bankrupt us.

Like I had so many times in the past, I meditated to find the right path forward. That's when I heard this: "God is going to send a message to Arpo. He has been treating people unfairly for a long time. You're going to be an instrument. You better get used to this. This is the way the material world works."

I shared this with Lila, as she was still my business partner in Pacific Spirit, and she understood, but we were still very stressed and worried. The day of the trial arrived, and Lila and I took our places on each side of our lawyers. Before the trial began, I looked at Lila and noticed that she was praying. I was, too. Despite the growing divide between us, I was glad to have her by my side during this ordeal.

When the judge called the court to order, the entire courtroom started to shake. It felt like an earthquake. Lila and I leaned back in our chairs and looked at each other, silently mouthing, "Lord Narasimhadev," an incarnation of Krishna known as the God of Justice. Apparently, we had both prayed to this form of the Lord.

Our trial started on Monday morning, and for the next five days, we heard insult after insult and lie after lie from the opposition while the judge, literally, slept. Still, the charade went on.

By the time I took the stand, I had hit a breaking point. The lawyer asked me a question, and I just started to cry. I wasn't crying about what was asked of me, I was crying because of everything I was going through—Lila's affair and our divorce, the unraveling of Pacific Spirit, and now this court case. I was still battling my heart issue. God had told me He was using me to send a message to someone else, but I struggled to believe in the promised outcome.

The judge decided we had to wait until Monday for closing statements. That weekend was the longest I had experienced since being charged with five felonies and twenty-three misdemeanors when I was only twenty years old.

On Monday morning, Arpo's team was feeling confident. His attorney asked the jury to consider raising the charge beyond $8 million. "Something to the tune of $24 million," he suggested. Our attorney, on the other hand, made one simple request: just be fair in your decision and base it on something that you could live with should you ever meet either of these two gentlemen on the street. Then, we broke for the jury to deliberate.

When the jury returned, we faced our moment of truth.

As the jury shuffled back in with their verdict, I couldn't help but think about how I thought I was through with this sort of thing in my life. But here I was again, my future in the hands of a small group of people who were to judge me based off a few short answers and the lies of those who had hoped to line their pockets with my bad fortune.

Even if the jury was to award Arpo just $1 million, we would have to shut Pacific Spirit's doors and sell our home. I was scared.

I took a deep breath in and the head juror began to speak: "All charges are to be dropped against Mark Kenzer, Naomi Sakanoue, and Pacific Spirit."

What a relief.

But he wasn't through.

Much to the astonishment of the opposing team, Arpo was charged with fraud and fined $125,000 to cover what he owed us for the overbilling, plus some of our attorney fees.

Arpo appeared to grow smaller and smaller as his attorneys gathered up their yellow notepad spears and their black briefcase shields and headed out of the courtroom. He wasn't going home with $8 million. All he could take with him was his deflated ego.

We never did see the money that was awarded to us. Getting it would require going back to court, and with everything I'd already been through, I decided that just wasn't worth the cost.

FRIENDLY BETRAYAL

While the outcome of the lawsuit was positive, the deceit and betrayal didn't stop during this time of my life. Friends and colleagues—people I trusted with everything I had—would prove to let me down, too.

After the lawsuit ended, Lila and I continued trying to make the best of our bad situation. We agreed to work together to try to keep Pacific Spirit going—if only for our team and the nonprofits we funded abroad. But it was a struggle.

The truth is, I wanted—and needed—someone who could help me run my end of the business. And who better to do it than one of my oldest friends, Jerry?

Jerry, you'll remember, was the cousin of my childhood friend, Jeff, and was always very business-minded, albeit not the most successful. Jerry had been the one to get me started in the jewelry business decades ago, and he'd also invited me, and then myself and Lila, out to New York to help with his various businesses. He played an instrumental role in reigniting my entrepreneurial spirit.

And, as it turned out, Jerry was looking for work at the time when I needed help the most. He had been working for Riviera Trading, selling sunglasses, and he had been making a lot of money doing it. But for some reason, he lost that job.

I trusted Jerry—we'd been friends most of our lives—and he knew my personal situation and what was happening with Lila. He became the perfect choice for me to bring into Pacific Spirit to take over some of my duties.

We weren't just becoming business partners. We were becoming roommates.

Just before reconnecting with Jerry, I had left the farmhouse and I moved in with my then-girlfriend, Brit. Brit was fifteen years my junior, and we were both going through a divorce. I knew moving in with her probably wasn't the best idea, but I had to get out of that farmhouse.

Then, Brit introduced me to her new boss. Immediately upon meeting him, I had the same feeling I had with Kurt and Lila. I told Brit I knew she was going to have an affair with that guy. She was appalled at the accusation. "No way," she said. She reminded me that he was fifteen years older than me and called me crazy.

Only one week later, Brit told me she was going to visit her mother and asked me to be moved out by the time she got back. I was right—she had gotten together with her boss. Another affair, another cheat. At least it happened before I grew too attached.

And so to Jerry's I headed, where he let me crash rent free.

The circumstances should have been ideal for me, but soon after we hired Jerry on at Pacific Spirit, our employees let us know this wasn't going to work out. From the offset, Jerry didn't seem to understand the business. He had spent most of his life as a sales rep, donning suits and ties and priding himself on his expensive wardrobe. Our business was on farmland, and everybody dressed very casually. But Jerry insisted on coming dressed in a suit and tie for at least the first day to make an impression. He thought that he was making a statement, and he did—but the wrong one for our employees. They said Jerry just didn't fit.

But I loved Jerry, and I wanted to give him a chance. Instead of pulling him aside, I doubled down. Soon, I had turned most of my daily activities over to him and trusted that he was carrying them out as I requested. And for the most part, he was, except for one small thing. As with Arpo, it all came down to money. Over the course of the year that Jerry worked for Pacific Spirit, he embezzled more than $30,000.

I can't begin to tell you how shocked I was to learn this, and how hard it was to tell Lila, who had only agreed to hire Jerry because he was my friend and needed work. But it was even more difficult to confront Jerry.

As painful as it was, at least Jerry didn't try to explain his way out of it. He didn't lie to my face or disappear, and he didn't try to sue me. He rectified the situation, but we had to let him go all the same. Thankfully, I had already moved out of his house, having decided I needed to learn to live on my own.

Since that time, Jerry and I have remained in touch but only slightly. Our once-close ties were mostly severed.

Another close friend gone—at the moment I needed them most.

Jerry wasn't my only business-minded friend who would betray my trust. I would experience another letdown with my business colleague, Abdel.

I met Abdel at the Tucson Gem Show. He was a wholesaler, and before I went into his tent, I had a feeling immediately that we were going to do a lot of business. But we got off to a rocky start. At the show, he told me that he didn't even have time to discuss business with me. Instead, he invited me to come to his showroom and warehouse in Los Angeles.

So Lila and I did. It was during that conversation that our friendship was forged. As we told Abdel about Pacific Spirit, its mission, and our adventures, he excitedly asked if we had gurus. This wasn't the sort of thing that was common at that time, and we didn't want to put him off, so we gave him a vague, deferred answer.

"Because I'm a disciple of Paramahansa Yogananda," he said.

I was shocked—and relieved.

"Well, Abdel, so am I!" I said.

"We're God-brothers!" he cried happily, and the connection grew from there.

For years, Abdel and I cultivated a business relationship built on trust and camaraderie. Abdel owned a business called International Gems and Minerals, and he would invite me to go on buying trips with him—like the catastrophic trip to China Lila and I would make with him. For these trips, we'd front him money for first rights to whatever he brought back. He'd always been good with our money. I'd loaned him up to $400,000, and it was all paid back with interest.

Our relationship extended beyond business, as well. Abdel gave me emotional support when I had first learned of Lila's affair, and he had been there for me when she finally came clean and divorce was the only way forward.

Abdel was also there in the moment when Lila and I finally realized we couldn't salvage Pacific Spirit and needed to sell the company. After years of trying to keep the company airborne, we simply couldn't do it anymore. This was especially difficult for Lila, whom I suspect had wanted to keep our marriage together precisely so we could maintain the company. We had always been romantic and business partners, and she had tried (very clumsily) to maintain the business partnership while ending the romantic one.

Her efforts were for nought. The company had failed.

And there was Abdel, eager to buy.

He asked me to come down to Los Angeles to meet some business partners of his, Kirk and Teresa. They ran a successful online business and wanted to buy Pacific Spirit alongside him.

I agreed. I had every reason to trust Abdel in business, so I assumed I could trust his business partners, too. However, when Abdel, Kirk, and Teresa came up to Portland to do due diligence, see the products, and sign contracts, Lila and I felt significant reservations about the sale.

As Kirk and Teresa reviewed everything related to Pacific Spirit, Lila and I pulled each other aside. "These guys don't know what they're doing," we said to each other. We decided we needed to warn Abdel.

We told Abdel to be wary. "They don't understand what we do. We don't think they can run this company," we told him. "We think you should pull out of the deal. We can find another buyer."

But Abdel was adamant, "No, this guy is a genius," he said of Kirk.

"We're telling you as a friend, don't buy the business," we reiterated. We really wanted to sell it, but our concerns for our friend came first.

"You trust me, don't you?" Abdel replied. "Don't worry about it. They'll cover it, and if they can't do it, I'll step in."

With our fears brushed off, Abdel, Kirk, and Teresa signed the main contract to buy Pacific Spirit, and Abdel signed a separate personal guarantee. Jesús and I had fourteen days to ship a million dollars worth of inventory to them. They got everything, and we got a little money each month in return.

But within a few months, I noticed things didn't seem to be running as they should be.

I called Abdel. "Where's the catalog? I'm looking at the website, and nothing is trademarked. They aren't protecting themselves or using the names properly." Once again, my concerns were brushed aside.

Then, I got a letter in the mail. Kirk and Teresa were declaring bankruptcy. After that letter came the calls from Abdel. He became extremely angry. He accused me of putting him in a difficult financial position. He'd curse me and claim he didn't have to pay. Eventually, he even tried to charge me with elder abuse, saying that, as he was in his seventies when I sold Pacific Spirit to him, I had manipulated him and created this whole situation.

When that happened, I felt something snap in my gut. This was Abdel, a person I had grown close to and loved, but elderly abuse was a very serious allegation.

I pushed our long-time lawyer, Mike, to take this to court.

"Abdel has got to back down," I told him. "He knows he's lying."

Abdel would indeed back down, but not for a while. Instead, his side pushed the litigation aggressively despite having no real case. Abdel and Teresa were lawyers. The original contract had been drawn up by Kirk. There was no way Abdel was unaware of what the contract said.

Finally, Abdel realized this as well. He dropped the case, and he agreed to pay us back over time with interest.

This could have been another lost friendship in my life, but months later, I made a fateful choice in writing Abdel. I told him that I still considered him a friend.

Then, the call came. It was Abdel. "Will you talk to me, Mark?" he asked. "I'm in southern Oregon. I'll drive wherever you want."

We met in Eugene.

"I'm so sorry I traded your friendship for money," he said. "I knew I shouldn't have listened to the attorneys, but I did."

To make it up to me, he took me to Egypt, a trip he'd promised for years. I was so glad to have the old Abdel—my friend—back.

Mark in Egypt

Abdel and I remain in touch to this day, even though Abdel, who is now in his eighties, has taken a slightly different path than me. Abdel at one time had wanted to be a monk, and I always remarked how transcendental he was. But he has largely abandoned his spiritual path in this life and chooses to focus strictly on business. Still, we have deep love for each other and always will.

In the wake of so many betrayals and losses at this point in my life, my friendship with Abdel reminded me that despite misunderstandings and mistakes, relationships can be repaired, especially when you remember that life is really about love. I would continue to see that as I confronted mending one relationship I had long deemed irreparable—the one with my father.

HEALING AND LOSS WITH MY FATHER

Growing up, I hated my father. I had always imagined beating him up when I got big enough. I couldn't wait to be sixteen and beat the hell out of him the way he beat the hell out of us. When I did finally get big enough, though, I couldn't do it. In the end, he was still my father.

Instead of fighting him, I tried to find ways to love him. When I first started therapy, I tried to bring my father along on my healing path. I'd try to hug him, and he'd push me away. We never had much of a conversation, mainly because we didn't communicate, we argued.

In the '80s, my mom dragged my dad to Marriage Encounter, a faith-based marriage program, and that seemed to create a crack in his stony mask. They went away for a weekend, and he learned that his emotions weren't wrong, he simply was avoiding them.

But soon thereafter, Dad covered that crack up. Even when Ross died, he didn't really show any emotion. He'd struggled with Ross coming out as gay, and he'd never been able to create that close relationship. I knew Ross's death must have been painful for him, but he wouldn't show that pain to anyone.

It took my mother's death before he began to finally open up. After she left her body, he became much gentler with me. It wasn't just gentleness, either. He finally put some effort into building a relationship. Every time I was leaving the country, I'd go down to Los Angeles to see him before I left.

He still had trouble listening, and that structure he had been raised with that held him back remained, but he was making an effort. We were making progress.

Then he met his second wife.

Dad called me one day and said he was getting married. I'd never met the woman. I knew he was dating—he loved to dance, and I knew he would pick up women in his dance class—but I didn't know he was serious about anyone. As far as I know, she just appeared.

Once I did know about her, I did not like what I learned. Hazel was a hairdresser with three divorces in her background. She had an old station wagon and a lease on her hair salon. She claimed she didn't need his money. She claimed she had plenty.

I told him he should consider a prenup. He laughed it off.

A few years after they got married, though, Dad got sick. Suspiciously sick.

He developed a mysterious, rare form of cancer. He also developed dementia. My father—the same person whom I had only seen sick perhaps twice in my life—suddenly was dying.

To make matters worse, Hazel refused to get my father treatment and convinced him there was no treatment for his condition. She even had the audacity to tell my brothers and me that she hoped that he would die, that she was sorry she married him.

When I called my father the day before he was to die, I could hear Hazel in the background yelling that she was leaving. My father informed me she was leaving on vacation with her friend. They were going on a cruise ship to gamble—while he was at home *dying*.

The next day, Hazel's daughter, Kirsten, called to tell me that my father had passed away in the night. It took Kirsten days to track down her mother and convince her that she needed to come home from vacation.

She didn't want to take a break from the party to bury her husband.

My brothers and I would sometimes comment on how they deserved each other. And there were more than hurt feelings behind these comments. Hazel was clearly manifested from my father's own rotten karma. He had been an indifferent husband and a poor father in this life. He may have been as bad or worse in previous lives. I hope Hazel's mistreatment burned off that karma for him before he enters his next life.

Unfortunately, Hazel did not disappear from my life after Dad left his body. With Dad gone, Hazel had control of Dad's will. She had changed our family trust before he died without his conscious approval. With our trust money in hand, she proceeded to go on a spending spree, burning through millions of dollars on high-risk investments and extravagant vacations for her and her friends.

The party was just getting started for her.

My brothers and I agreed to let this go. There wasn't much we could do, after all.

About a year after my father's death, though, we received a court notice that Hazel was trying to grab stocks that my father had left to us. This, we decided, was just too much. We filed a lawsuit, although it got us seemingly nowhere thanks to a judge who insisted we work it out ourselves.

Despite mounting legal fees, we kept the pressure on.

Finally, some progress was made when Hazel decided she no longer wanted to pay her big-shot Hollywood attorney and hired a new lawyer. After reviewing the case, he revealed to Hazel that the trust didn't actually belong to her—she was listed as the income beneficiary, meaning she would receive income from the trust until she died, but she did not control it. This is what my father had told me when he was coherent.

My brothers and I had finally gained back some control, but the damage had been done. While Hazel agreed to make the trust whole, millions of dollars held within it had been spent or hidden by Hazel.

What's more, our petitions to get the money back remained ignored and unread by the judge. I would come to have a whole large file drawer filled with these petitions as the judge would continue to put off a decision for years.

This was a very painful battle, and at the end of the day, it wasn't really about money—it was about principle.

We'd grown up poor. Our father never encouraged us; he'd never given us love and support. He'd been jealous of his wife and his sons. He'd beaten his children, and he'd ignored my mother in her greatest moment of need.

The one thing he'd done for us was work hard and pull his family out of poverty—leaving a great deal to his sons to build our lives on. The home my parents created and that money had been our only comfort, and in some sense, our consolation. Our father had failed to provide love, but he'd provided us security.

And Hazel was taking it all away.

In this situation, I felt the same powerlessness I had during my other court cases—from the charges from my jewelry business to the copyright suits. I had this sense that somebody else controlled my life. And all I could do was stand by and wait to see what happened. I know Dad wouldn't have wanted me to feel that way.

It's funny, in a way. In my youth, my father would always point out cheaters to me. He was hyper-aware of scams. Yet, he seems to have fallen for one in the end. And his sons kept paying for it—for years after his death.

CONSOLATION THROUGH LOSS

Amidst so much negativity surrounding me, I found comfort and needed perspective in the words of others, including my friend, Bill Welch.

I met Bill when I hired him as my therapist, at the suggestion of a friend. But when I showed up for my first session, it was clear we had a friendship connection. Bill offered me a choice: I could see him as a therapist or we could be friends, but we couldn't be both.

I had lost quite a few friends at this point, along with my former best friend—Lila. I decided I could use a new friend more than a good therapist, so I chose that.

I was giving up a very good therapist, though. Bill didn't just follow the standard textbooks for counseling. He practiced the Diamond Approach—a spiritual process of waking up through knowledge of the Self. So, while he wasn't my hired therapist, his wisdom still played a large role in my life.

Once, when I was feeling particularly frustrated with the direction Pacific Spirit was trending, I said to Bill, "I am so sick and tired of being the Mystic Trader."

His reply, "You never were."

I just laughed. He was absolutely right. We all come to identify as the things in our life: our marriage, our kids, our job. But we aren't any of those things. I wasn't Pacific Spirit, or the

Mystic Trader, or Lila, or my relationship with my father or his money. Bill's words helped me see that.

On another occasion, Bill and I were walking through the forest talking about Lila's affair and the divorce when I said, "I never thought this would happen to me."

"Well, why not?" he responded.

Once again, he caught me. I'd grown up in a world in which this happened every day. I had even told my mom to divorce my father. Why had I assumed it couldn't happen to me? I had come to simply believe my thoughts. I was so conditioned to think I was different. I may have been more advanced in my spiritual perception, but I was still playing an active role in the material world. And material existence is filled with the sort of pain I was experiencing in this period.

This was the point of the *Bhagavad-gita* when Krishna and Arjuna confront killing all of Arjuna's kinsmen. Krishna tells him he must face this calling; it's what he's here to do. Krishna says:

> "Do thou fight for the sake of fighting, without considering happiness or distress, loss or gain, victory or defeat—and, by so doing, you shall never incur sin" (Bg 2:38).

He then goes on to add:

> "You have a right to perform your prescribed duty, but you are not entitled to the fruits of action. Never consider yourself to be the cause of the results of your activities, and never be attached to not doing your duty." (Bg 2:47).

Through his words, Krishna told Arjuna he couldn't back down. He had to participate in his part in the cosmic play. These men were to be put to death by Krishna; Arjuna was just an instrument. All of this was already done.

I, too, had been an instrument. God had said as much in the case against Arpo. But it was equally true in my case against Hazel and indeed in many actions throughout my life. I am not special in this. We are all instruments of God. Jesus himself, in saying, "There is no good but God" in the New Testament was an instrument for God.

Wisdom at this time also came to me from one of the most unsuspecting sources—Rama.

In those years of tension between Lila and me, things had also been tense with Rama. It was no more than his youthful need for independence, but it was yet another relationship that had grown distant.

When Lila came clean about the affair, she insisted on telling Rama by herself. She took him outside and told him what had happened and what was going to happen.

But when Rama came in after talking to Lila outside, he came up to me and said something very profound:

"You know, Mark, material life is inherently meaningless. I suggest you find something that you love. For me, I love music. I'm fortunate because I can use that to fill my time. If you don't have something you love, you better create it, otherwise you'll be very unhappy."

I took his words to heart. I would spend years finding—and creating—that happiness again. It would not come all at once, but it would shape the next stage of my life—and it would eventually lead to my third awakening.

BATTLING THE GRIM REAPER

Three times in my life I've had to fight off spirits trying to take over my body and my spirit. The first time occurred in a dream. I was walking in a dark jungle and saw a puppet that looked just like a wooden human being. It held out its arm and when I was close enough, it jumped into my body and tried to take it over.

I yelled out to Krishna for help. When I woke up, I patted my body to make sure it was still mine.

The second time, I dreamt I was in a Latin American country. I went to a bar and walked over to talk to the bartender. A woman at the bar leapt into my body and took over. We did battle.

I could feel myself losing control of my own body. Panicking, I shouted, "What do I look like?" I grabbed hold of my beard. "I have a beard. I am a tall man." I had to describe myself to gather the strength to take my own form back.

Jolting awake, I ran to the bathroom and looked in the mirror to see if I was in control. I could still see her in my eyes, sharing my body.

The encounter reminds me of Matthew 10:28, "And fear not them which kill the body, but are not able to kill the soul: but rather fear him which is able to destroy both soul and body in hell."

The third battle was the fiercest. The first two had been possession, this one was a battle with Death personified. I truly fought for my life in a grueling brawl. After a long fight, I finally overcame him. But then, Death outsmarted me once again. He smiled and turned into a baby.

I had to laugh. I couldn't defeat him. He beat me by starting the cycle of life over again.

This is what material life is like. It's what we go through, but it's not what or who we are.

We can never outsmart death; we can only overcome him by truly accepting this truth.

Jesus said he'd build the Temple up in three days. He was talking about the three sheaths of the body: the physical body, the mental body, and the subtle, or causal, body. If you want to overcome death, you have to free yourself of all attachment as you face Death.

As Jesus cautioned, "And truly I say to you, you will not come out from there until you give the last quarter cent" (Matthew 5:26).

This is not easy, as I learned from my mother.

When my mother first entered Heaven, she came to me in a dream to tell me how great it was there, that she could get anything she wanted. I told her: "You're only experiencing your good karma. When the good is used up, you'll start experiencing all the negative that has been left undone."

There is a balance of dual energy. We must take the good with the bad, the positive with the negative.

Once we are out of this body, we can use our karma any way we desire, but once the positive karma has been used up, the negative will still be there. That is why the Vedas recommend that we transcend the positive *and* the negative.

A few years later, Mom appeared to me while I slept.

"Mark, I'm feeling depressed," she said. "There isn't anything for me to do here. I feel as unhappy as I felt on Earth. I don't know what to do or why I'm here."

She had failed to find balance in her karma. As good as her heavenly experience had been, her hellish experience was equally bad.

So long as she continued along the same course, she would cycle through this process forever. Heaven and Hell. Life and death and rebirth. The only freedom comes from laughing at Death when he plays his game—and accepting that we can't win at his game. We have to free ourselves from the game entirely.

CHAPTER 12

ANOTHER AWAKENING

RAMA WAS RIGHT. I HAD TO FIND SOMETHING I LOVED IN this material life.

But that was a deep and intense struggle. At the time, when I was getting divorced, I could barely do anything, let alone find love. I would often get in the car to go to work and find I couldn't do it—the same way I couldn't take a flight. It was all because of my heart. I couldn't even go to my job because of my broken heart.

One day while driving, a voice dropped down upon me.

"You are not a victim," it said.

"Oh, yes, I am," I replied out loud. After a moment, though, I started to repeat what I had heard, "I am not a victim."

After saying it a few times, I asked why this was true.

I was totally surprised at the answer. It burst upon me like a flash of lightning. If you are a victim, you'll never take responsibility for yourself. You are giving your own power away.

I was not a victim, I decided. I might not like what is happening, but I was not a victim. This was my karma, good and bad, and I had to deal with it. Nobody was going to fix it for me.

I walked into my office one day, and like usual, there was a stack of sample products on my desk. We received these a lot from artists and the like wanting consideration for placement in our catalog.

One of the samples caught my eye. It was a recording of poetry by Hafez, the fourteenthth-century Persian mystic and poet. When I left the office that day, I decided to pop the CD into the player in my car for the ride home. As I drove along, I wasn't sure what I was listening to, but I noticed that I was no longer feeling bad. My blood pressure was normal for once. I was actually feeling a great calm.

I paid closer attention to the words of the poems. At first, I didn't grasp the meaning, but then I let my heart listen, and I became transformed. Before long, Hafez became my Sufi guru. I was so moved by his words. It was as if he had written these poems just for me. He knew that we all had to suffer deeply. He was a voice with balm for our wounded hearts. I listened over and over to the same CD. Whenever fear took over and my blood pressure soared, the heart-soothing words of Hafez eased my burdens.

One evening, I sat down, alone with my despair. Instead of reaching for a volume of Hafez, I picked up a pen and pad to write my feelings. Instantaneously, I began to write poetry. It came to me like an automatic writing. This was the first time that I had written a poem since my high school days.

The next morning, I picked up the pad and read what I had written:

I ran to check the trappings of my love,

but my cage was empty.

I will come again,

If need be a thousand times,

until my restless mind finds stirrings of your presence.

Did I really write this? It was so simple, yet I was moved by it. It had hardly made sense the previous night, but today, it revealed to me a secret: I could once again feel love.

Poetry became my new love. I was in love with this new voice I had found. Finally, I felt hope that I could come out from the shadows of my past and move into the light of my future.

At first, I was a bit shy about writing these spontaneous, heartfelt writings, but soon, I found myself penning them each night. As soon as I was settled in my bed, that inner whisper would again speak to me, *pick up a pen and write*.

I had no idea what was going to come out, but write I would. Then, the writing would stop, I would put down my pen and paper, and I would go to sleep. There was no need to read it then, it wouldn't make sense until the morning.

This was my first finding of love, as Rama suggested. It helped get me through those long, sad nights as I learned to be alone, with no one but God.

FINDING LUCINDA

I had found love in poetry, but I still longed for love in another form—that of female companionship.

Lila's affair had left me feeling lost sexually. I felt like something had been taken away from me, although I couldn't put my finger on what, exactly. As a result, I found myself looking at any woman for a sexual relationship.

First there was Brit, the young yoga instructor who left me for her older boss.

And then came Julie. Whenever Julie touched me, it felt like she was mothering me. When I told her this, she grew upset. But the next day, she called me and asked me to come over. She'd had a dream in which she'd given birth to a newborn and when she looked into its eyes, she realized the newborn was me.

Julie had been my mother in a previous life. She and I got along well, but that wasn't quite the connection I was looking for.

Next came Danielle. Danielle and I had a spiritual connection—she even had a dream once about Ross before she knew he was my brother. However, the more time we spent together, the weirder Danielle grew. I had let her move into my house with me, and eventually, I had to move out of my own house to get away from her.

Once again, not the relationship I sought.

Finally, I met Lucinda. Lucinda was the owner of a local used bookstore at which I would attend a poetry group. Lucinda was quiet, reserved, and intelligent, and I found myself wandering into the store just to talk to her. I simply liked being around her. Plus, she wrote amazing poetry and really enjoyed mine as well.

I finally built up the courage to ask Lucinda out, only to find that she was starting a new relationship and moving an hour away. I felt a prophetic stirring and immediately knew it wasn't going to go well.

I looked at her and thought to myself, "Oh, that's going to go badly. I guess I'll see her in seven years."

Seven years. What a long time to wait. "We'll both be sixty!" I thought.

But we kept in touch when she moved away. I congratulated her when she and her new boyfriend opened a bookstore in their new town. Then, three years later, he died of cancer. Lucinda was deeply depressed.

"You have to get outside of yourself," I advised. "You want to go for a ride on my motorcycle?"

She loved it. This quiet librarian and bookshop owner delighted in the thrill of riding on the back of my bike. And that woke up those feelings that had existed between us all those years ago.

We grew closer during this period of mourning. Finally, Lucinda and I got together, almost exactly seven years after my prediction.

HEALING OLD WOUNDS

While the events of my material life were raging chaotically, my spiritual connection and ability to make predictions remained steadfast.

While Lila and I were still married, a friend asked if I wanted to buy his mother's beach house. I remember standing outside of the house with Lila saying, "Oh boy, I'm going to own this house one day."

How odd it was then to suggest that *I* would own it and not *we*. Yet, eight to ten years later, I actually bought it.

But I didn't want to buy the house all on my own. So, I turned to the person I had been doing business with for years— Lila. Even though we were divorced, I asked if she wanted to purchase it with me.

It was a natural decision, despite our troubles. Even as our lives separated, we never made a complete separation in business. At first, it was because of our employees at Pacific Spirit.

But truthfully, as much as I wanted a clean break, I couldn't do it. We were compelled to have some connection. As I told her once, "When you leave your body, you'll find that we are together eternally on some level—no matter how painful."

That prophecy might seem romantic, but it was just as much a curse. We were tied together, no matter what. As much hurt as she had caused me with her affair, it was clearly painful for her to see me start seeing other women.

For a time, Lila used that beach house with Kurt. Then, I stayed there, fulfilling my prophecy that the house would one day be mine. After we sold it, we had to figure out what to do with the money. Instead of investing in a new business or setting it aside, Lila found another property: a run-down eight-plex.

The place was disgusting, but Lila wanted to make it nice and make it work for people who needed a home but wouldn't normally qualify to rent this type of place. It'd be another way for us to provide for others. I liked the idea. So Lila and I bought the eight-plex and remodeled it to be high-end without kicking anyone out, except for the crack addict living there.

People these days love to flip homes, but as with everything in our career, Lila and I were pioneers. It became another one of my loves—something to occupy my time and allow me to do good in the world. And, it kept Lila and I together in some capacity. This was all the more important after Pacific Spirit closed.

At some point, there was an easing of the pain in my and Lila's relationship, and we fell into the new form our connection would take for this life.

As the pain from my divorce from Lila began to fade, I decided it was finally time to tend to another lingering ailment:

my heart issue. I would never be able to live my life as fully as I hoped if I constantly feared dying.

I spoke with Lila's brother, Brian, who was a doctor. He told me about a talk he'd attended given by a young doctor, Dr. Randolph Jones, who specialized in correcting the exact condition I'd suffered with over the past twelve years. He handed me the doctor's card and suggested that I give him a call.

Twice in the past I had met with doctors who promised they could fix my heart issue. Both times, they offered me a pacemaker. But I didn't want to be fixed in that way; those doctors spoke to me like I was a car with a dodgy engine. I knew people who had those operations done, and they still lived on daily medications, never fully returning to their former selves. I didn't want that for myself if I could avoid it.

I met with Dr. Jones with those previous experiences in mind. If I even heard the word "pacemaker," I was ready to walk out the door. After reviewing my records, though, he told me he was 95 percent certain my condition could be corrected with ablation. He said we could do the procedure within two days.

Suddenly, I felt apprehensive. I had lived my life staying away from medical doctors as much as possible. While I had overcome much of the inherited trauma from my mother and my experience with the doctor who first treated this heart issue, I was not entirely comfortable with this decision. *You will die* no longer echoed in my brain, but fear still resided there.

I mentioned this predicament to Bill Welch, and in his usual wise, therapist-friend fashion, he offered simple words that resonated with me.

"Why wouldn't you do it?" he asked.

He was right. Why *wouldn't* I do this? Ninety-five percent was almost perfect. And the alternative was becoming increasingly unbearable. I couldn't live like this any longer.

So I called and made the appointment. I have no memory of the operation, but I was told it was a success. And since then, I haven't had a single issue with my heart. Now my heart functions like everyone else's.

Another form of healing came with the final resolution of the court case with Hazel over my dad's estate. If I learned anything from that experience, it's that justice is blind and by no means swift.

We hired a fearless and honest litigator, Benazeer (Benny) Roshan, who helped finally put Hazel in her place. I was appointed successor trustee, and Hazel received monthly income and the right to live in our father's home until she passed away in 2021.

After eight years, we had a resolution.

Remarkably, this was my fifth victory in court after facing impossible odds. For the fifth time, there was deliverance. The first had been my father's case over the slot machines; the next three were mine—over the jewelry business, our trademark against Whole Life Expo, and the case against Arpo for Pacific Spirit. This fifth case was both Dad's and mine and, finally, it brought us together.

It was a powerful moment of healing that, like my repaired heart and repaired relationship with Lila, left me more whole.

SEEING MY PARENTS AGAIN

Since getting divorced, I'd been going to therapy when things got to be too much for me. I'd found a Hakomi therapist named Lisa Maeckel who would get me in during times like this, and she was very good at what she did. Hakomi is a holistic approach to therapy that merges ideas about mindfulness and nonviolence inspired by Eastern thinking. The practice—and Lisa—were perfect for me.

One day, Lisa asked me to close my eyes and just be present. To my surprise, my father appeared in front of me. He wanted something.

Dad walked up to me and climbed up to stand on my shoulders. Then, his father arrived and climbed up to stand on my father's shoulders. My grandfather's father came next, and the generations of Kenzer men kept coming.

"What is this?" I cried out. "I'm not doing this anymore!"

I took an abrupt step sideways to the left, and they all came tumbling down. As they fell to the ground, I could feel that they all carried similar hurt in their hearts—the pain, abuse, and genetic dysfunction that had been handed down for generations in our family. It needed to stop. I had refused to hit Rama, so the energy was now lying dormant. I told my father we could put an end to it once and for all with forgiveness—and love.

And that's just what we did. I offered my love to all of them. It poured out of me—right there in my therapist's office.

I felt strong and independent. I could sense who I really was, not who I'd become conditioned to be. Lisa suggested that I pay attention that night to see if this was over. I knew myself and if there was something more to be worked out, it would come to me in a dream.

And it did. That night, I had a dream that I was a monk in India, with a clean-shaven round head and a bright yellow robe. I saw a group of eleven other monks gathering, and I joined them. Once we were all seated, the head monk started discussing who amongst us was to be the one who could lead them and humanity into the future.

One of the monks looked at me and said, "Now that you've obtained a state of love, you must open up and share it with all." The leader was to be me, everyone was in full agreement.

As I looked around at the monks, I recognized a few of them

from my current life. What was strange was that they, like me, had much different bodies, heads, and faces than I had been familiar with in this life.

Suddenly, it dawned on me: this life as a monk in India was my real life. The life in which I was sleeping was a projection or an extension of this reality.

As we monks had gathered near a forest grove, I saw many people lining up to get our blessings. As they made their way to me, I noticed they floated just above the ground and wore flowing chiffon gowns. One by one, village people came up to each of us. I glanced down the line and saw a man and woman I recognized: my parents.

My mother came up first. She expressed just how much she and my father had loved me. She then looked to my father as a way to encourage him to express himself. Then, my father opened up, "I don't know what to say, but I love you. I love you. I love you. I love you."

I could see that this was a big step for my father to open up and I reached out to pull him closer into me. I could feel his pain.

"This is good that you can let this go," I said as we embraced. I told him I loved him, too.

Then, he let go and held up his hands.

"This is all I can handle at the moment," he said, giving me one last smile that conveyed such gratitude as he and my mother moved on to the next monk.

It was a moment I had longed for my entire life, yearning for my father's love, whether I knew it or admitted it. It seemed the vision in Lisa Maeckel's office removed whatever obstacle had blocked the flow of love through male generations of my family. It freed my father to finally communicate that love, and it enabled me to see this vision of my true life.

This was the last time I saw my father, but I knew where he was. He'd come to me once before in a dream.

A few months before my father had died, I asked him if he was scared and what he thought was going to happen.

"I assume I'll just go to sleep and not wake up," he replied. "The lights will just go out."

I reminded him about my vision with his father and shared with him that since that time, I had similar experiences with others who have passed on.

"Well, we'll see," he said skeptically. "I hope you're right." It was obvious he was afraid and that it was unpleasant for him to be dying.

When my father passed away, all of the conflict and anger that I had felt between us for most of my life passed away as well. The strain that came from negative mental, emotional, and physical energy dissipated once he was no longer embodied. A few months after his death, my father came to me while I was asleep. When I saw him, the first thing I said to him was, "You're dead," to which he replied, "Where is it that I'm dead?"

Oh right. He was dead in my reality, not his.

I realized that we were living in different dimensions, but wherever my father was, he was fully awake and more animated than I ever remembered him being. He showed me the beauty of where he was. He spoke about being free, of all the wonderful places he had already been, and all the places he still planned to visit. As he described these beautiful vistas, I could also see the colorful intensity of the heavenly realms as these images were also being transferred in vibrant detail into my consciousness.

I told him I wanted to go with him. He just smiled, looking as if he understood something that I didn't. Before he could say anything more, I said, "Wait! Let me go get my passport! I'll go with you." He gave me the same look and nodded. "Okay, Mark, you go get your passport."

So I did. Then, I woke up laughing.

Since these visions, my love for my father has been more intense than I could have ever imagined. From a childhood and adulthood spent hating him, I have such unbelievable love for him now.

At times, the love is so intense, it feels like the ecstatic experience I had when I was first with Lila and couldn't stop chanting the name of Chaitanya Mahaprabhu. Or the overwhelming love and joy I felt during my first awakening.

It was like a whole river of generations of love from my family had been dammed up. Now that it flowed freely, the current of love grew powerful and radiated from within me.

LOSS DOESN'T GET ANY EASIER

Despite the more positive path my life was taking, I was not protected from the pains of material existence and the loss of those close to me.

Revatinatha, Revati for short, was one of my closest friends. Tall and long-haired, he wore a beard, which was very rare for a man who was part Native American and a Hare Krishna.

Shortly after we met, Revati let me know that like me, he was also a follower of Paramahansa Yogananda, and even accredited Yogananda with saving his life. Revati went on to tell me that in his younger days, he was a mountain climber and that he had fallen off a high cliff, and fortunately for him, he remembered his then-guru Yogananda praying on his way down. Due to the damage that was caused to his spine, he now stood about two inches shorter, as he pointed out, had this not happened, we would have been the same height.

For several years, Revati would help us at Pacific Spirit during the holiday seasons, and everyone appreciated his kind and sweet disposition.

One afternoon, however, I could see something was bothering him. He looked depressed.

Revatinatha

"Revati, what's going on?" I asked.

He just laughed like he usually did.

"Everyone else may think that you are a jovial guy," I continued, "but I can see that you're very sad inside. You are no different than me. What's going on?"

Revati was one of the few people that I knew personally who was very well read in scriptural sciences, had some very deep realization, and actually tried to practice what he read. Most saw him as one of the happiest people they knew. But I could see something was eating at him deep inside. I recognized it because I, too, had something eating at me most of my life. I could never put my finger on it. It was buried deep within my soul.

"You're right," he confessed. "I have so many people who tell me how much they love me, but they don't know who I am. They don't even care to inquire. All they see is that I am happy on the outside and that is enough for them. I appreciate that you can see me as I am."

This conversation opened up a new area to our relationship, and he admitted that, lately, his life somehow or other had become unmanageable. The next afternoon, the subject of suicide came up. Revati asked me my opinion of it. I answered as honestly as I could.

"In my earlier years, I thought suicide was wrong and, for the most part, unnecessary. Now, I don't think suicide is much different from any other type of dying—it's a tragedy for those left behind," I said.

There's a saying that when we are born, we cry and everyone else is happy. But when we die, we are happy and everyone else cries. This is the duality of this world. Death is death. And whether you take your own life, die of disease, or die in a car crash, you're still going to be the only one that is going to have to deal with the experience and also how you move through it. Everything is temporary, and everyone must fly their own plane.

That was the basis of my belief on suicide, and I explained that to Revati. Then, I asked him what he thought.

"I think the same way," he said. "Why would it matter if we are in this body or another? People are only interested in us sticking around because they don't want to face the fact that death is just around the corner for everyone. I really don't think it matters. We are just conditioned to believe suicide is wrong because it's what society teaches us."

Later that same evening, Revati and I continued that same conversation, and I began to really feel Revati's pain. Perhaps I had said the wrong thing at the wrong time. Suicide may ultimately be the same as any other death, but life is precious and for us to live. I did not want to lose my friend.

The following morning Revati and I met at my house and we drove together to Pacific Spirit continuing our previous conversation. Later that afternoon as we drove back, I tried to get Revati to open up. We then sat in my car for two hours talking about his pain. But no matter how hard he wanted to say what was going on within, he couldn't bring himself to open up fully.

For me, it was a very uneasy two hours. I suggested we go inside, but Revati insisted he needed to get home. So I tried to keep him talking in my car.

He revealed he had made out his will and left everything to his daughters.

He had prepared.

The feeling of death standing over me started to become unbearable. There was a heaviness similar to what one might feel watching another being led to their own execution.

"Revati, promise me that you will go see someone," I said desperately. I recalled a conversation I'd had with Bill Welch about Revati only days before. "I have a friend who's a therapist, and he is willing to see you right away. I have already spoken with him about money, and it's not an issue."

Though he appreciated the offer, Revati insisted on leaving, saying he needed to go see his daughter.

"Promise me that you'll come back and speak with my friend or that you'll find a qualified person to speak to," I reiterated.

I could feel him slipping away, and I grew very concerned this was going to be our last time together. Revati promised and headed down the road.

The following days, I sent Revati some emails. No response.

My heart sank. I could no longer feel his presence in this world. *Was he gone?* I kept asking myself, but I had no reason to believe that he wasn't going to return like he said he would.

I tried calling. No answer.

All I could do now was cry. Despite my spiritual growth and the wholeness that was returning to me, it wasn't going to be any easier letting go of someone I had loved so dearly than it had been in the past.

The next day, I received a card from Revati in the mail. The image on the cover was a Native American dream catcher with a white dove flying through it. Revati had placed a beautiful feather inside and written the words: "My brother. Sometimes the words just don't say enough. Thank you."

I cried so much. My friend, like the dove, had flown and was on the other side of the dream. A few days later, I received a call from a mutual friend informing me Revati had taken his life.

I sat in disbelief, feeling the shame of not holding onto him just a little bit longer. That feeling of powerlessness that each of us must come to terms with in this world was, again, a reality for me.

A little over two years after his death, Revati came to me

in a dream. Of course, I was most curious about what he had gone through, what he learned, and most importantly, how he was doing.

"It was very difficult at first," he told me. "And I was in some heavy darkness. I was in a lot of pain and had to work very hard to get released from it. But now everything is okay, and I'm doing much better. Can you let everyone know that I love them? And that I am happy?"

That was all I could hope for my friend. And really, that's all I ever wanted for any of the loved ones I'd lost—my mother, my father, Dan, Bob, and my brother Ross—was to know they were at peace in the life they now lived.

We all suffer in this life, and most of us at one point or another think about ending that suffering. Most of us move through this period, but some do not. In the end, it didn't matter how each person I loved and lost died, I still endured pain from the separation I felt at their death. I still grieved for their loss in this material existence. Their happiness in the realms beyond me was precious, but I couldn't help but long for their presence again.

That's the reality of temporary material life—pain and suffering; loss and longing. Even amidst positivity in so many aspects of my life, I still experienced it. There was no escaping it. It is simply part of existing.

SHARING TRANSCENDENCE

Following the devastation of Revati's death, I tried to once again refocus on the love I was creating in my life. Though I had lost another friend, I still have my ecstatic poetry, Lucinda, and my renovation work. Another form of love I had come to cherish was the gift of setting others on the path to God.

Shortly before the divorce from Lila, I was talking with one of our closest neighbors, Preston Alexander, who lived with his wife and two kids exactly one mile from our property.

"My wife wants to open up a New Age store," he said. "Would you be willing to come and talk to her?"

That next evening, I was invited over and met Pam for the first time. She was short, but you could see she had a large heart. It was written across her sweet, mischievous, freckled face with its green eyes and loving smile. Pam and I immediately hit it off, although I am sure that most people, when they meet Pam for the first time, feel that connection. Pam is one of those people who has a huge heart, and you can't help but feel love coming from her.

Mark and Pam in India

I sat on one side of the living room with Preston and Pam on the other. Though I was there to advise Pam, Preston quickly took over the conversation. He had a science background and talked about all sorts of things, but he never once mentioned the fact that Pam was interested in a career and consciousness makeover. He clearly was not spiritually minded like Pam. In fact, he could be outright dismissive of spirituality.

"All I ever wanted to do was love God," said Pam as soon as Preston left the room to get some tea.

"I think I can help you," I replied softly.

Once Preston was back, I could feel the energy totally shift back to his science-minded talk.

I listened to what Preston was saying, because, as a spiritually minded person, I was still raised and lived in the material world. I didn't feel threatened by his conception of the universe. It could be very elucidating in its place. I understood what he was saying, even if I didn't know the terms. This is the case of most people with a spiritual bent—we can understand the materially minded side of things, but materially minded people don't usually understand us. It was always the same thing with my dad (in his material life) and my older brothers.

Though Preston's conversation was warm and entertaining, I could tell Pam and I weren't going to get very far addressing her interests on that night. So, I told Pam to give me a call later.

The next day, she did just that. Finally alone with her, we could discuss what had brought her to me. It turned out, she had been living quite the out-of-body life, unbeknownst to her husband. If she was to go deeper into this, I suggested she involve Preston, but Pam said she'd tried. Pam said Preston saw everything as a mixture of chemicals—nothing more. He didn't believe in God.

I couldn't say I was surprised.

A skeptical nature isn't necessarily a barrier to spiritual development, but Preston seemed unable to take the leap from science to the Divine.

Where to me or Pam, everything is about love, Preston wanted proof of the love. He told me it was just a reaction of chemicals. He saw nothing beyond the molecules. It's just how he was wired.

Pam was tired of putting aside her own spiritual journey for him. She said she just wanted to love God. She wanted the real thing.

In Pam, I had an ideal student. I had long worked with eager fellow journeyers. I had taught a class on the Bhagavad-gita at a night school in Portland and elsewhere. I had also given personal classes to Kurt and Susan, as I had for Dan and Jan. As Pam's realization deepened, we were becoming lifelong friends. She was so eager to learn and progress on her path. I enjoyed sharing this sacred wisdom with her.

I suggested that we study the Bhagavad-gita together. Soon, we were also studying Srimad Bhagavatam.

It's hard to communicate the speed of her advancement. As far as Vedic text goes, the Bhagavad-gita is the first book that is suggested. While one can spend a lifetime trying to fathom the depths of its wisdom, on the surface, it is very clear, precise, and easy to grasp. It's a high-school level spiritual text.

This is not to diminish its beauty or spiritual power. It is perfect and complete in itself, and it is most sufficient in delivering one back home to God.

The *Srimad Bhagavatam* is considered college material and actually takes one's consciousness from where the *Bhagavad-gita* has laid the groundwork and opens doors into higher realms of realizations. The *Bhagavad-gita,* with its seven hundred verses, is very concise. The *Srimad Bhagavatam,* on the other hand, has eighteen thousand verses and threads through the reader's consciousness—opening the reader up to new thinking and then dropping them off at God's doorstep.

In short, if you want to know who you are in relation to God, read the *Bhagavad-gita*. If you want to know who God is and how you live in the world and reciprocate God's love, then read the *Srimad Bhagavatam*. Both are transcendental literature. Pam was not done. She asked about *Śrī Caitanya-caritāmṛta*, the biography of Chaitanya Mahaprabhu. It is very rare that someone in the West would be attracted to the teachings of Lord Chaitanya, especially someone with a Christian background. But to me, the book is more than it appears to be on the surface. It's about waking up one's dormant love for God. And for Pam, it was much the same. *Śrī Caitanya-caritāmṛta* is the voice of not only liberation but of loving Divine association directly with the Supreme. There's nothing higher in transcendental literature and in transcendental knowledge. This is a graduate-level sacred text, and Pam and I were journeying through it together.

As Jesus said, "For where two or more are gathered in my name, there am I with them." We could feel that Divine presence in such moments.

I was ecstatic to have someone so close to share this book with once again. In the same way that Lila had shared this nectar with me, I was sharing it with Pam. Taking one's spiritual life seriously is the highest goal of human existence. As Lahiri Mahasaya, Yogananda's great guru, used to tell his disciples, "Everything can wait, but your search for God cannot wait."

The more reconnected Pam became with the Vedic understanding of spiritual life, the more she wanted to visit India. Years later, I was able to make that desire a reality when I won two roundtrip tickets to India from British Airways. Pam had since divorced from Preston, and I knew now that it was the time to take Pam on her journey to the holy land of Vrindavan.

Vrindavan is said to be one of the most holy cities in India. It is said to be a replica created by Krishna of His home in the spiritual world. Everyone there is a devotee of Krishna or Rad-harani, the female energy of Krishna, or both.

On this trip, with my heart repaired and my soul full of expectation, I had no fear. There was no crisis at the departure gate. No phone calls or Divine intervention was required. I was simply a devotee taking another devotee to one of the holiest places on Earth.

Or, as Lord Chiatanya might say it, I was merely the servant of a servant of the Divine.

The evening Pam and I arrived, it was clear that no matter how tired we were from our travels, we weren't going to rest now. Vrindavan was alive with hundreds of thousands of pilgrims from all over the world. They were here to celebrate Karthik, which occurs every year in October or November. Devotees of Krishna hope to associate directly with the Lord during this time, and many believe they will be awarded liberation from the material world by pleasing Krishna or Radharani and their devotees.

Pam and I slowly made our way through the throngs of pilgrims to the Krishna Balaram Mandir temple. Even if you weren't a devotee of Krishna, you couldn't help but feel the love. As we entered the main temple, it was filled with close to a thousand worshippers. Most sang the Kirtan. Some were crying and many were offering small ghee lamps. As usual, men and women were divided on their respective sides inside the temple.

Pam made her way near the front so that she could get a better look at the deities on the altar. I stayed back and started praying to Lord Krishna. From the intensity of everyone's prayers, my heart started to melt. I became overwhelmed and tried to hold back inward emotions.

I felt a deep sense of love and joy for Pam. After a lifetime of searching, Pam had finally returned to the Divine. It had taken decades of searching, years of study and devotion. She had traveled around the world because of the love and faith she held in her heart. In a way, Pam had known that she was coming home to a place where she must have lived in a previous life.

I prayed, "Dear Krishna, please give Pam some mercy."

The crowds pushed forward and the temple priest began removing the flower garland from the deities. Everyone who was close enough to the altar reached out, hoping to receive this special mercy of the Lord. I slowly made my way through the crowd and watched as the temple priest handed a very large, beautiful garland to a man at the front.

After he accepted the garland, he turned around, holding it in front of him in both hands, as if he was going to place it on someone. In that instant, our eyes connected, like he had heard my prayer. There were at least fifty devotees between us. His eyebrows raised in question and, understanding that he was acting as God's messenger, I pointed to Pam, whose back was facing me. The devotee walked over to Pam, glanced back at me to ensure he had the right person, and then proceeded to place the garland over the back of Pam's head.

Pam, of course, didn't know what was happening but could feel the charge of this action. Suddenly, the women around Pam came to get pieces of the Lord's mercy. Pam broke the garland while it was still around her neck and, as quickly as she could, handed the flowers to all the women around her. She then turned to me to see if I had seen what happened.

She had a huge, childlike smile on her face. Tears welled up in both our eyes. At this moment, Pam tasted what we had been reading in the texts we studied—the difference between mundane and transcendental love. It's rare to experience this in our material life. Surrounded by struggle, sorrow, and the temptation of material reality, it is difficult to attain this type of love of God.

And Pam, through spiritual fortitude, was experiencing it in front of my eyes.

For me, it was the first time I had shared my spiritual wisdom with someone and helped them cross the bridge into the spiritual world while still in the midst of life. Dan had crossed that bridge at the end. Revati and my parents had found it after death. I had attempted several times to help others take that step—Staz, for example, and Ross—and found they lacked the strength or inclination to follow. Something held them back. This was the first time I had taken the hand of someone eager to learn and led them to their spiritual destination.

Now, Pam and I were experiencing direct association with the Divine through the Mercy of Krishna. I had helped bring her to this moment, and we experienced the joys of that journey together.

THE THIRD AWAKENING

After experiencing the pleasure aiding Pam along her spiritual path, I decided to go through the *Bhagavad-gita* and *Srimad Bhagavatam* and highlight all the verses that could lead to awakening. I reread both texts and marked each verse, but this led to a dilemma. How best to communicate and share this wisdom?

I decided to start a blog. Each entry contained a verse, along with commentary I wrote about that verse, along with supporting documentation and references from the world's scriptures and words from men and women of science.

I did this every day and felt a connection and responsibility to do it. Even if I got home at midnight, I wouldn't go to bed until I'd posted at least one verse.

I realized that I was doing this because I felt a responsibility to Krishna Dvaipayana a.k.a. Veda-vyasa. He is called the literary incarnation of God because of his contribution to texts we now all read and study. He is regarded as the author of the *Mahabharata*, the longest epic ever written, and also the compiler of the mantras of the Vedas and of the eighteen Puranas and Brahma Sutras. Many consider him to be an Incarnation of Vishnu. I have felt indebted to Veda-vyasa ever since the first time I read the *Bhagavad-gita*. This debt to his great gift for humanity had been nagging me since a previous lifetime.

My blog found a receptive audience. Many of my readers were Christian. By now, I'd come to see that my role was not unlike Yogananda. I was to speak to receptive Christians about the greater truth of our spiritual existence. It was clear from Rama's choice of Jesus as a guru, Dan and Jan's seeking out classes with me, and Pam's childlike smile at the Krishna Balaram Mandir temple.

The followers of my blog were similar to all of these individuals. They were so open to hearing this wisdom because they could feel that connection between Jesus and what they were reading, just as I always had. It was fitting that just as Jesus called me, my words called to many of His followers.

Once I finished this process, I published these collected posts in a book, *Awaken Into Enlightenment*. Immediately after publishing it, I experienced my third and final awakening in this life. Everything fell away, and I felt no draw to continue my spiritual practices.

I felt like an empty vessel, but this was not an unpleasant feeling. I felt as if I had finally crossed the ocean of material suffering and that there was no longer a reason, having arrived on the other shore, to continue dragging the boat behind me.

Now, when I pray to Lord Jesus or Lord Shiva, I no longer desire to be like them. I used to hold them up as an example of what I could and wanted to become. Since "waking up," I recognize that all I can possibly be is who I already am. Certainly I can progress, learn, and develop spiritually. But I am no longer trying to walk someone else's path. I have embraced the truth behind my stories. When the story is seen for what it is, the energy around it dissipates, and all one is left with is who they have always been. There is nothing to add or take away.

I continue to live this life, meditating and moving through my journey, but I feel a distance from it. I realize now that I'm being lived, not living, and I have been integrating back to what some call "true nature." What is that true nature? I'm just an instrument of light—a son of light, if you will. There is no more to me than that. I continue to spread these truths and channel them back to others, but I do not seek much beyond that effort. After a lifetime of turmoil, I am at peace.

LICKING THE OUTSIDE OF THE JAR

In India, they say that we all want to taste honey, but it's in a jar. For the most part, we waste our time licking the outside of the jar, unless a guru opens it for us. That's what Lord Chaitanya did for all while he was in his body—he distributed the honey of love freely.

We are all capable of opening the jar without a guru, but once we are conditioned by material life—by the example of our parents and the demands of everyday existence—we lose this knowledge. We cannot just connect to the love of God as we are meant to. If it was that easy we would already have done it. Instead, we try to satisfy ourselves by glancing at the honey that is out of reach and licking the glass in the futile hope that we will somehow get a taste of what is within. No matter how intelligent we are, we can act like dogs, licking the outside of the container.

I have made this same error. I was conditioned by my father and mother, who had lost the path to God. Like others, I have been lost in material obligations—focusing on work, paying taxes, and taking nice trips.

It is all so much licking of the jar. But it is possible to learn, once again, to open it, if we have eyes to see and ears to hear.

CONCLUSION

I HAD A DREAM IN WHICH I WAS WITH GOD. GOD HAD A form like something Gary Larson would draw for his comic strip, The Far Side. He was massively tall—much larger than the average man—with long hair and a big, white flowing robe. We stood with other men and women, also wearing white robes, all on a hill. I don't know where I was, but it felt like Israel.

There were big baskets of primitive bread rolls, and we were to distribute them to the masses of people down in the valley below.

God spoke to us as people shouted up for their piece of manna. We were going to throw it down to them. Then, God pulled me aside and said, "Don't go all the way to them. They must meet you at least halfway. They have to make some effort to come to you."

In society today, we've become so entitled. We don't want to make this effort. We want the manna thrown down to us where we are.

The dream reminded me of a line said by Jesus, "Don't cast pearls before swine."

The wisdom of enlightenment is only for those who work for it. One needs to decide if they want to just improve their lot in the material world or completely free themselves from the continuous cycles of birth, old age, disease, and death.

You've taken a few steps up that hill by reading this book. Reading through my story, you may wonder why the quest for God and the Eternal Self has been so miserable. It may strike you as odd that someone who has seen the future, who has received writings from God and saints, and who has dreams with departed souls should somehow continue to suffer the same difficulties as the rest of the world in my material life.

The answer is as simple as it is, perhaps, unsatisfying. I suffer because we all suffer. Material existence is suffering. We are, none of us, as central to God and existence as we feel. In fact, the trappings of our lives are only temporary—on some level, they are distractions from what and who we eternally are. To transcend these distractions, we must understand the true nature of our reality.

As A.C. Bhaktivedanta Swami reminded his disciples, "The pains and pleasures of the body are not the pains and pleasures of the soul."

It is said that a seeker once approached the Buddha, asking whether he was an angel or a god. The Buddha replied, "No." The seeker then asked if he was some sort of saintly person or a man. The Buddha again replied, "No." The person asked, "Well, my friend, then what are you?" To which the Buddha replied, "I am awake."

And to be awake is to realize what we are and what we are not. Jesus once said that the meek will inherit the earth. What he meant was that those who recognize how little they truly possess are the ones who will truly know reality.

You may be Mr. or Mrs. So-and-So with this spouse and these

children, and this house, car, and job. But none of this is you. You are not even your body. Those things are real—they exist, they connect to you and happen to you—but they are not you.

All you are, all any of us is, is love, Spirit soul, and its desire to create. That creative impulse is God's force within us. According to the Vedas, the universe came into being when God was lying on a Causal Ocean, the origin of the material creation outside of time and space, breathing out multi-universes within His dream state. And as He dreams, multiple universes are woven into creation. Planets burst from him and populate the skies. All living and nonliving entities are a part of this creation.

We are a part and parcel of God, a part of His Dream State, but we are not the Absolute. And the people, objects, and pleasures we surround ourselves with do not belong to us. They do not define us, nor do they come with us further on our journey.

The Vedas caution that the most dangerous thing is to think that you've become God. That's what's happening now in many spiritual movements. People realize their oneness with God, but they confuse that with being God. But we do not own any of these things in material life. Nor do we control any of this.

Whatever you have, you have to give it up. That is the key to taking your next step up the hill—a step in which we reintroduce the Absolute into our daily lives.

While loss was painful in my life, I was only able to advance so far because of that loss. It was only through realizing that I was not my parents and not the husband of Lila or father of Rama—that I was not the Mystic Trader or jewelry store owner—that I could see who and what I really was.

With this perspective in mind, I encourage you to reread this book. Focus more attention on the spiritual lessons at the end of each chapter. Seek greater understanding through the example of my suffering and my triumphs.

My goal in writing this book is to have met you halfway. This path is not an easy one. We are all like fish out of water. We struggle and flop around. If someone picks us up and places us back into the water, everything is all right. This is the job of the Spiritual Master. Like Jesus and so many others who have pointed the way, I hope that you take just one step closer to the water's edge. Come on in, the water's fine!

Once you have finished this book, I suggest you continue your journey through the *Bhagavad-gita*, the *Srimad Bhagavatam*, or my book, *Awaken Into Enlightenment*, that condenses and comments on some of the most important verses from these texts.

Take heart from the knowledge that whatever path you are on is the right one. Ultimately, only you can take that next step. Seek the truth, for, as Jesus said, "If you abide in my word, you are truly my disciples, and you will know the truth, and the truth will set you free."

This freedom comes only if you are willing to incorporate it into your life and live it fully. I wish you a successful journey.

ABOUT THE AUTHOR

MARK KENZER was the founder and CEO of Pacific Spirit Corp. He built a multi-million-dollar business from $300, met with some of the greats in eastern philosophy, and traveled the world. Through Pacific Spirit Corp, he published two main catalogs, "The Mystic Trader" and "Whole Life Products." After undergoing much suffering throughout his life, Mark became God-realized.

Made in the USA
Columbia, SC
19 June 2023

17964210R00155